A COVENANT TO KEEP

Meditations on the Biblical Theme of Justice

James W. Skillen

CRC Publications
The Center for Public Justice

We wish to thank Susan Weaver Van Lopik, coordinator for justice education and advocacy for the Christian Reformed World Relief Committee (CRWRC), for writing the "Justice Happening" stories at the end of each theme section.

Unless otherwise indicated, the Scripture quotations in this publication are from the HOLY BIBLE, NEW INTERNATIONAL VERSION, © 1973, 1978, 1984, International Bible Society. Used by permission of Zondervan Bible Publishers.

Scripture quotations noted from the RSV are from the HOLY BIBLE, REVISED STANDARD VERSION, © 1952, Thomas Nelson, Inc. Used by permission.

Cover illustration by Chet Phillips/© Artville.

We welcome your comments. Call 1-800-333-8300 or email us at editors@crcpublications.org.

Library of Congress Cataloging-in-Publication Data
Skillen, James W., 1944–
  A covenant to keep : meditations on the biblical theme of justice / James W. Skillen.
    p. cm.
  ISBN 1-56212-544-3
  1. Christianity and justice. 2. Justice—Biblical teaching. I. Title.

BR115.J8 S58 2000
241'.622—dc21

00-037892

10 9 8 7 6 5 4 3 2 1

ACKNOWLEDGMENTS

Most of the meditations included in this book first appeared in the *Public Justice Report* in a column called "The Testimony." I am grateful to staff members, trustees, and members of the Center for Public Justice who read and kept encouraging me to write that column and who now support the publication of this book. I especially want to thank Carol R. Veldman Rudie, long-time friend and trustee of the Center, who urged publication of this volume and offered many suggestions about how to do it. Finally, thanks to Marlene Brands and Robert De Moor of CRC Publications for their investment of editorial energies in this project. Above all, may God be praised!

James W. Skillen

CONTENTS

PREFACE

This study of the biblical theme of justice is intended for small group and personal use. It is especially aimed at social action groups within the church or larger faith community.

The format centers on *five essays* which explain how Scripture confirms that justice is required, restrained, administered, assured, and fulfilled. Each of these five concepts is further developed in a set of fifteen meditations, for a total of *seventy-five meditations.* We suggest that small groups use the essays for study and discussion, perhaps over a ten-week period or longer, and that the meditations be used for personal reflection during the weeks between meetings.

Each essay and meditation concludes with two or three *questions for group discussion and personal reflection* and with one *suggestion for doing justice.* Some activities (prayer, financial support, and so on) can be carried out from the comfort of your armchair, while others encourage community involvement and other forms of more active participation in the political system. Recognizing that no one person or group can do all of the activities suggested, we recommend that you choose one or more activities that groups or individuals can carry out over a period of time.

We trust that you will be challenged to look at justice from a more in-depth biblical perspective and to increase your involvement toward the fulfillment of justice in God's kingdom.

Bob De Moor
Editor in Chief
Education, Worship, and Evangelism Department
CRC Publications

THE BIBLICAL DRAMA

In the past God spoke to our forefathers through the prophets at many times and in various ways, but in these last days he has spoken to us by his Son, whom he appointed heir of all things, and through whom he made the universe. The Son is the radiance of God's glory and the exact representation of his being, sustaining all things by his powerful word. After he had provided purification for sins, he sat down at the right hand of the Majesty in heaven. So he became as much superior to the angels as the name he has inherited is superior to theirs.

—Hebrews 1:1-4

PROLOGUE: THE BIBLICAL DRAMA

G od begins and completes all things. The Lord speaks, and
creatures appear. The Almighty touches dust from the earth, and
human history begins to unfold. The heavens testify to the divine
majesty. Flowers and fields breathe the Creator's name. Children
playing, farmers cultivating the fields, teachers teaching—all point to
the one who made us in the divine image and who, in these last days,
has spoken to us directly by his Son. The one who creates and upholds all things, the one whose glory, beauty, and love inhabit the
creation, governs all things wisely and justly.

God's wisdom and justice have everything to do with human
government and politics. Political life at each point in history—from
the smallest legal detail to the greatest achievement of any earthly
kingdom—tells something about the ruler of heaven and earth.
Nothing within the ambit of human political life occurs outside the
reach of divine authority, and everything moves toward the climactic
disclosure of creation's meaning in the Day of the Lord.

This world—our world—is God's world. It is the gift of God's
creative joy, the arena of the Master's deepest grief, the pathway along
which the Savior walks to accomplish God's purposes. Consequently,
in each generation, in each new century and millennium, those to
whom the Creator has given the special charge of earthly stewardship
need to remember what God has already accomplished even as they
look forward to what is still to come.

Mysteriously, God's promises—sealed in covenants made with
men, women, and children—define history and drive it toward the
ultimate revelation of the City of God. God's covenants embrace
more than politics, of course, but political life also finds its place, its

only place, in the all-encompassing drama of the Lord's covenanting purposes.

To read the Bible and history aright, therefore, is to see and to hear the covenant Lord keeping his promises. This *Covenant to Keep* drama does not occur as only one act or one scene in a larger play; it is the play, the entire production. Sun and moon, sand and sea, plants and animals, angels and humans all find their place in a single drama. The whole cosmos, from origin to fulfillment, exists as the garden and the workshop, the temple and the city, of the Lord's revelatory purposes.

The Son through whom God has spoken with historical finality is the One through whom the Creator first spoke in establishing this complex cosmos. The One who radiates divine glory among us has sustained it all from the beginning. And in the fullness of time, the Son of God, mediator of all creation, became one of us in our human generations, stooping as the Son of Man to offer purification for our sins. For that sacrifice and humble offering of his life to the Father, God appointed Christ heir of all things. After he was raised from the dead, Jesus Christ, fully human, fully divine—and now representing countless human brothers and sisters as joint heirs—sat down at the right hand of the cosmic Majesty to reign forever and ever as the King of kings.

Since this is the meaning of our world, any attempt to abstract government and law from God's covenantal dealings with creation through Jesus Christ only twists and obscures their true meaning. Consequently, we should read the Bible and examine politics not as if we are the ones who must establish the connection between them, but rather with the understanding that God's word creates, defines, sustains, judges, and fulfills human political life from beginning to end. The political world is not a closed human territory. It is a revelatory arena of double entendres: God's authority, whether expressed in judgment or in blessing, reveals itself here and now through human government on earth, and at the same time, human governments always point ahead, in anticipation, to the climactic fulfillment of Christ's governance of the City of God.

JUSTICE REQUIRED

"In the beginning, O Lord, you laid the foundations of the earth, and the heavens are the work of your hands. They will perish, but you remain; they will all wear out like a garment. You will roll them up like a robe; like a garment they will be changed. But you remain the same, and your years will never end."

—Hebrews 1:10-12

W hen God spoke and the creation appeared, it turned out just right. Heaven and earth, the first plants and animals, and the first of the human generations all came into existence precisely as the Creator desired. The covenantal drama dawned brilliantly. Everything was very good. The Lord of heaven and earth rested on the seventh day in the confidence that all was in order.

God saw all that he had made,
and it was very good.

—Genesis 1:31

The apostle John, like the author of the letter to the Hebrews, tells us something more about God's creation of the world. The entire cosmos has been made through the divine Word who was with God from the beginning (John 1:1-2). The apostle Paul confirms that the Son of God, who became incarnate as Jesus Christ, is the mediator of creation. In the act of creating, God did not toss the universe into an impersonal void. No, the creation was fashioned in and through God's Son. The creation exists within the hospitality of this divine communion.

Revealing God

The creation story makes this point in another way: God's original order for all things is seven days, not six. The creation comes from the Creator and has been destined for fulfillment in God's sabbath rest.

The creation reveals God through the Word of God and exists for the Lord's ultimate satisfaction and joy.

For by him all things were created: things in heaven
and on earth, visible and invisible, whether thrones
or powers or rulers or authorities; all things were
created by him and for him. He is before all things,
and in him all things hold together.

—Colossians 1:16-17

God demonstrates this truth again and again. When the Lord brought the Israelites out of Egypt, they were not simply sent on their way. The Liberator walked with them and showed them day after day that they were living in God's very presence. The Redeemer tabernacled with them, fed them, and led their trek across the wilderness by pillars of cloud and fire. God did not simply drop in on the children of Israel from time to time; they lived within the hospitality of God's own communion, and the Lord was leading them toward the ultimate sabbath rest of God (Heb. 4:6-11).

The creation is a single, comprehensive order of diverse creatures who exist within the divine communion. Every creature has a role to play in revealing and praising God.

The Creator makes and blesses each creature for specific purposes so that together they may dance in the delight of revealing the divine glory. Creaturely diversity is not a haphazard chaos but a symphonic wonder. Each creature has its own glory, its own role to play in God's complex drama.

He makes the clouds his chariot and rides on the
wings of the wind. He makes winds his messengers,
flames of fire his servants.

—Psalm 104:3-4

An Awesome World

Many times in my life I have been awestruck when seeing one of God's creatures for the first time. God made millions of kinds of plants and insects and sea creatures and animals, each with distinct habits, a unique appearance, and different habitat. And God made humans capable of creating many different cultures.

The variety of food prepared and eaten in various cultures around the globe is just one of the evidences of human imagination, talent, and creativity. Recently when traveling in Korea (the first non-Western country I had ever visited), I was amazed by the food. It is completely different from Western cuisine. How can people across the world create so many different kinds of food? We can do this because God places creativity and diversity within us and empowers us with curiosity and wonder about everything around us.

The grand symphonic complexity of God's creation cries out for recognition and celebration. Each creature, because it is God's, calls for special recognition and honor. Every creature, in other words, deserves justice so that the entire creation can testify to the glory of the Lord.

Who Can Do Justice?

How can each unique creature receive justice—its proper respect and due regard, its fitting treatment and honor? Who can do justice to God's creatures? Since the creation displays God's covenantal purposes, who besides God can exercise responsibility for the well-being of so many creatures? Who besides the Almighty can do justice to the world?

The amazing answer to these questions is that the Lord of the universe has placed all creatures except one under the care of that single exception. The Creator gives humans responsibility for one another and for all other creatures. The Lord, who both requires and exercises justice, has granted earthkeeping responsibility to the creature whose peculiar identity is to be the image of God (Gen. 1:26-28; Ps. 8). God does justice *to* the world, in part, by commissioning human beings to exercise justice *in* the world. God gives human beings their proper due—their proper respect and honor—by making room for them to exercise a responsibility that might seem to belong only to God.

Think of something as delicate and risky as caring for a newborn baby. God gives adults life-shaping power over their young—over the very image of God. Or think of the overwhelming power of nuclear weapons, which can destroy life on earth. God gave humans the capacity to understand how to make and use such weapons. God put the world, and the divine communion itself, at tremendous risk by giving humans so much responsibility.

The demands of justice, therefore, come with creation. Everything about the meaning of justice reaches back to the original rightness of God's seven days in which human creatures are called to be stewards and caretakers. God's creational purposes place their demands on humans in every arena of life. All of the Lord's judgments and blessings throughout history reaffirm God's first covenant with Adam and Eve. God's judgments against sin and God's redemptive actions in Jesus Christ do justice to, and fulfill, creation. From the beginning to the end of the seven-day drama, God requires justice.

The LORD reigns, let the nations tremble;
he sits enthroned between the cherubim,
let the earth shake.

—Psalm 99:1

Even though one day the creation as we know it will change, to be rolled up like a robe and brought to fulfillment in God's presence, the Creator of all things will remain the same. God's demand for justice will never expire. And one of the great mysteries about creation is that God's exercise of justice will honor and fulfill, not abrogate, human responsibility to do justice.

REFLECTING . . .

- When you hear the word *justice,* what comes to mind? Even though it is difficult to define justice, make a list of some of the characteristics you associate with justice and injustice.

- Why should Christians think of justice as being grounded in God's purposes for creation?

- Why is it impossible to imagine that God's creation could be fulfilled without justice being done?

ACTING . . .

- Think of a specific contemporary personal, social, or political instance where you believe justice is not being done. How does this situation demonstrate injustice? Who bears responsibility to right the wrong—an individual, several persons, an institution? What would those involved have to do to restore justice? What role can you play?

JUSTICE HAPPENING

Who can do justice? Who must do justice? Jean Claude Cerin, a Haitian Christian, learned about the implications of these questions in 1997 while observing Christians in North America advocate to their own government at a national advocacy group's convention.

While realizing that actions that seem easy in North America may not be risk-free in the developing world, Jean Claude was inspired to explore the possibility of individuals and organized groups "doing justice" in Haiti. How, he wondered, could Haitians even dare to approach those in power in Haiti about the situation there? "I learned at that event about the working of civil society in the United States. The idea of the people holding representatives accountable for what's happening was an important lesson." Rather than complain about what was *not* happening, Jean Claude felt encouraged that he could work to remind the government of what it had *already* promised.

Jean Claude went back to Haiti with this important message. He acted on what he had learned, forming a coalition of Christian organizations to hold the Haitian government accountable for promises they had already made in their constitution and in their laws. Pulling people together in the living room of his home, Jean Claude shared what he had seen and inspired others to act with him to create change.

Who assures that justice is carried out? A person! The people! From fear to action, Jean Claude moved himself and others in Haiti to stand for justice. Today, a coalition of Christian Haitians is in dialogue with their government because one person saw a possibility.

MEDITATIONS 1-15

- 1 -

WHICH WAY FORWARD?

Jeremiah 6:1-21; John 14:1-21

The headline of a poster I saw pinned to bus shelters and billboards as I walked through Berlin in 1990 read, "A New Way for Germany." A year after the wall had come down and communism had collapsed, discussions of "new ways" into the future never seemed to stop. The excitement across Europe was palpable.

But which new direction should Germany and Europe take? The question remains very much alive today, and not only for Europeans. Along which path into the future should the people of any country be walking?

After liberating Israel from slavery in Egypt, God gave them directions for their journey into the future, including fundamental commands by which to judge whether their actions were right or wrong. God also told Israel to practice certain rituals regularly to remind themselves and their children continuously of their Redeemer and Pathfinder. In the early stages of their journey into the unknown God led them in a remarkably visible way by a pillar of cloud during the day and a pillar of fire at night (Ex. 13:20-22).

Sadly, however, Israel developed the deadly habit of ignoring the signposts God gave them and moving off in wrong directions. In response, God sent prophets to warn and redirect them. Hundreds of years after the Exodus, God was still pleading with Israel to follow the path to life.

"Stand at the crossroads and look; ask for the ancient paths, ask where the good way is, and walk in it, and you will find rest for your souls."

—Jeremiah 6:16

Many years later, long after God had driven Israel into exile and then allowed a remnant of Judah to return to the promised land, a young rabbi appeared among them. With the authority of one who knows how to erect pillars of cloud and ignite pillars of fire, Jesus said to his followers, "You know the way to the place where I am going" (John 14:4).

But Thomas, one of his disciples, said, "Lord, we don't know where you are going, so how can we know the way?" Jesus answered, "I am the way and the truth and the life. No one comes to the Father except through me" (vv. 5-6).

God sent Jesus not just to prophesy and *point* the way, but to stand in the place of sinners and *become* the way. In bearing God's judgment against the sins of Israel and the whole world, Christ became our advocate to open the way of love and truth and justice, which leads to the presence of God.

The way forward to a new Europe, to a more peaceful Middle East, to a more just North America cannot be organized by careful planning or good intentions alone. Humans make history by following either false gods or the true God. One path leads to destruction. Only the way of Jesus Christ leads to life.

REFLECTING . . .

- How can civic responsibility be a path along which to follow Jesus?

- When and how have you experienced this connection?

ACTING . . .

- The next time you vote, ask yourself which standards of judgment you are using and whether those standards provide a dependable guide to public justice.

"I am the way and the truth and the life."

—John 14:6

- 2 -

GAINING A GLOBAL PERSPECTIVE

Isaiah 40:15-24; Colossians 3:1-17

There is much talk today about our shrinking planet, population growth, and the increasing interdependence of states and peoples. A few years ago *Time* magazine made the point about the globe being an ecological commons by naming the endangered earth its "Planet of the Year."

Where can we find a standpoint from which to see the entire world in correct perspective? Surely that perspective must take into account more than natural ecosystems. What about human history with its diverse peoples and cultures that find themselves increasingly interconnected but also increasingly diverse and often at odds?

Every viewpoint from which to consider the globe's unity and historical destiny must pass a severe test—the test of interpreting reality rather than manufacturing dreams. Islam, Hinduism, the New Age Movement, evolutionary progressivism, Judaism, Christianity— all face the same test of explaining the value, purpose, and meaning of the entire cosmos.

Hundreds of years before Christ, Israel's great prophet Isaiah proclaimed that only one perspective on the globe can pass the test. That point of view belongs to the Creator of the ends of the earth and encompasses not only natural ecosystems but all of human history. That is fine for Isaiah to say, you may be thinking, but how can human beings gain the Creator's perspective on this world? Who can pretend to stand where God stands and not be considered mentally deranged?

He sits enthroned above the circle of the earth, and its people are like grasshoppers. He stretches out the heavens like a canopy, and spreads them out like a tent to live in. He brings princes to naught and reduces the rulers of this world to nothing.

—Isaiah 40:22-23

From a strictly human point of view, of course, all things are relative and temporary. Generations come and go. Our cultures are particular; each of us sees things from a limited perspective. Moreover, disoriented by sin, our understanding of life is twisted and obscured. We are not God.

But God's word to Isaiah has taken on flesh in Jesus Christ. Through Jesus, we are lifted up beyond ourselves to see from God's point of view. God has become one of us to lift us up as eagles (Isa. 40:31) to soar with our Savior on high.

The apostle Paul explains that God has acted with saving mercy to relocate us in Christ. Jesus triumphed over death, ascended into heaven, and now sits at the right hand of God. God does not hide in unreachable transcendence but rather, in Christ, calls us to communion in the divine sabbath. In Jesus Christ we gain access to God's perspective of the globe.

REFLECTING . . .

- What differences do you see between a Christian point of view of this world and a viewpoint that assumes there is no perspective beyond the globe?

- What comfort does God's perspective give you when the world—your own or the global world—is in turmoil?

ACTING . . .

- The next time you read an article about global finance or the global environment, look carefully to see if the writer assumes that this is a closed universe or a universe open to God's point of view.

For you died, and your life is now hidden with
Christ in God. When Christ, who is your life,
appears, then you also will appear with him in glory.

—Colossians 3:3-4

- 3 -

THREE-STORY UNIVERSE OR SETTING FOR THE DIVINE DRAMA?

Psalm 104

Certain critical scholars say the Bible should be demythologized because its ancient authors held an unscientific view of the universe. Biblical writers believed that the earth, floating on waters beneath, was encircled by a dome with stars, sun, and moon above. Today, of course, we know better.

Yet to accept this supposedly scientific correction of the Bible demands that we accept a new myth, which goes like this: Once upon a time, there was a chance occurrence that brought the universe into existence. Among the curious things that evolved by chance from out of the chaos were human beings—strange animals who learned how to analyze the universe by developing abstract concepts of time and space. Eventually, many of these animals came to believe that the truth about the universe can be settled only by means of scientific thought. In keeping with this myth, these scholars decided that people ought to remain agnostic about anything that cannot be explained by means of the scientific method.

Now wait just a minute! Look at the Bible again. Take Psalm 104, for example. These are not the words of a scientifically trained engineer insisting on a spatially abstract, three-story universe. This is glorious poetry, filled with wonderful similes and stunning metaphors.

He stretches out the heavens like a tent and lays the beams of his upper chambers on their waters. He set the earth on its foundations; it can never be moved.

—Psalm 104:2-3, 5

Modern demythologizers have made the mistake of ignoring the poetry, abstracting the spatial elements from it, and then turning deaf ears and blind eyes to the drama as a whole. The psalmist is not practicing bad science with primitive tools. He is marveling about God's great drama—the drama of creation's unfolding, of human sin, and of God's unsurpassed glory that will endure forever.

Of course, scientific work plays an important role in human exploration and development of the creation. Through it we can come to understand many things that will help us know how to do justice to God's creatures. But there's more to knowledge than scientific knowledge, and even scientific knowledge should begin and end with an expression of awe before the Creator whose glory endures forever (v. 31).

Which will it be? Shall we accept the biblical story in all its richness or bow before the new myth about the preeminence of science? This question cannot be answered scientifically, of course. As for me, I choose to stand with the psalmist, who can feel the earth tremble at the Lord's gaze and can see the mountains smoke at the Lord's touch (v. 32).

REFLECTING . . .

- Why are the Psalms and the parables of Jesus filled with so many earthly metaphors describing God?

- What evidence do you see that scientific thought gets in the way of praise for the Creator?

ACTING . . .

- Read Psalm 104 and list all the different word pictures the psalmist uses to describe the work of the Creator. Then underline the ones that most help you understand why and how God requires justice to be done to the creation. Observe these works of creation in a fresh way on your way to work, while out walking, or when meditating at the kitchen window.

How many are your works, O LORD! In wisdom you made them all; the earth is full of your creatures.

—Psalm 104:24

- 4 -

OF NATIONS AND COVENANTS

Jeremiah 2:13-37; Hebrews 9:11-28

God's covenant stamped Israel as a special people, making them a sign among the nations. From the law and the prophets we learn that God's marriage to Israel was to be the means of divine blessing not only for Israel but for the whole world.

God's special covenant with Israel obviously presented the nations with a great challenge. In order to enjoy favor with the true God they would have to recognize God's unique revelation through Israel.

The challenge facing Israel was even greater. True humility for Israel meant recognizing that the covenant-making God was not their private god. God rules as the Lord of all nations, as the Judge of the whole earth. Thus, when Israel fell into habits of disobedience, acting as if God could be manipulated to serve their ends, God's anger flared. Jeremiah and the other prophets reminded Israel of the covenant's curses against their injustice and idolatry.

"Your wickedness will punish you; your backsliding will rebuke you. Consider then and realize how evil and bitter it is for you when you forsake the LORD your God and have no awe of me," declares the Lord, the LORD Almighty.

—Jeremiah 2:19

Israel's covenant status was not inherent in Israel but in God's relationship to Israel. When the children of Israel began to ignore the terms of their relationship to God, God had to bring judgment in accord with the covenant's terms. Of the nation to whom much is given, much will be required.

The history that followed Jeremiah's awful prophecies is well known. The Bible tells of God's destruction of Jerusalem and the temple. It also records God's promises to the repentant Jewish remnant that endured exile with the hope of experiencing God's redemption through the coming Messiah.

However, the covenanting God does not exist for the Jews alone. When Israel's Messiah came to fulfill all the terms of the covenant,

Christ made it clear that he was sealing an ultimate and eternal covenant between God and all nations. God's covenant in Jesus Christ is a covenant of justice established through the mystery of God's forgiveness and reconciliation of the world. It unites those from every nation who, by faith, look ahead, not behind, to the promised land, to the kingdom of God (Heb. 9:27-28).

The new covenant confronts the people of every nation with a great challenge. Through Jesus Christ, all gods of national pride and imperial conquest have been placed under judgment as false gods. The new covenant cannot be a North American covenant or a covenant with the modern state of Israel or with the so-called Christian West. God's promises to Israel and to all the nations have now been fulfilled in that son of David, son of Abraham, son of Adam, who is the Son of God, the Lord of lords. The everlasting covenant in Jesus Christ is not less political than was the covenant with Israel; it is more so. For Christ rules everywhere, completely, and finally.

REFLECTING . . .

- To what extent do you think the myth of God's special covenant with America has hindered Christian understanding of God's new covenant with all nations in Christ? Is this myth unique to the United States?

- How does this eternal covenant between God and all nations play out on Sunday morning in your community?

ACTING . . .

- Consciously note your attitudes and actions toward those with whom you live and work who are different from you in terms of national origin, religious preferences, cultural practices, and so on. What can you do this week to demonstrate that the covenant-making God you serve is not your private god?

For this reason Christ is the
mediator of a new covenant.

—Hebrews 9:15

- 5 -
WEIGHED AND FOUND WANTING

Daniel 5:1-24

"You're finished, king! It's all over. Yes, only minutes ago you felt like you were sitting on top of the world. Your dinner parties never ended. You took any woman you wanted. Your power amazed rulers everywhere. But it's all over now. You're finished."

Who could possibly speak so brazenly to Babylon's King Belshazzar and live? No one, surely. But amazing as it might seem, Daniel, the young Jewish exile who spoke so harshly, was rewarded in the end with a purple tunic and a gold chain and appointed as the third highest ruler in Babylon.

How could that have happened? Let's go to Babylon to find out.

King Belshazzar is throwing a wild dinner party and relishing his awesome power. One of his small pleasures this evening is drinking from goblets taken from Jerusalem by his father Nebuchadnezzar. Yet, powerful as Belshazzar is, he can never relax completely. He must keep abreast of foreign troop movements and rumors about anyone who might challenge his authority.

Suddenly, Belshazar is shocked to see a hand writing words he cannot read on the wall of his banquet room. (Today, a world leader might suspect that a foreign intelligence organization is using a new technology to perform this feat.) Belshazzar speculates that a higher power is at work.

Pale and faint, the king calls in his highest paid astrologers and enchanters and demands an explanation, but none can read the writing or interpret its meaning. Hearing the commotion, the queen enters and urges the king to call in the best consultant he can find. She recommends a man named Daniel.

"There is a man in your kingdom who has the spirit of the holy gods in him. This man named Daniel, whom the king [Nebuchadnezzar] called Belteshazzar, was found to have a keen mind and knowledge and understanding, and also the ability to interpret dreams, explain riddles and solve difficult problems. Call for Daniel, and he will tell you what the writing means."

—Daniel 5:11-12

Desperate to learn the meaning of the words, Belshazzar heeds the queen's advice and orders Daniel to appear. The king is prepared to pay a high price for the truth, so he offers Daniel a huge reward—a bribe, actually. Daniel, who knows that his powers have not been earned and that he has no right to bargain for their use, humiliates the king with his very first words: "You may keep your gifts for yourself and give your rewards to someone else. Nevertheless, I will read the writing for the king and tell him what it means" (v. 17).

Recognizing his own vulnerability, the king overlooks Daniel's insult and waits to hear the interpretation. A proud and mighty king begins to bow before the higher power that has struck fear into his heart.

REFLECTING . . .

- In what ways has God exposed the pretense of some modern kings, dictators, prime ministers, and presidents?

- Whom can you identify as a recent or contemporary "Daniel" who has spoken the truth to one in power?

- How was Daniel's position both similar to and different from that of a Christian in any modern state today?

ACTING . . .

- Identify a situation in which you are subject to an authority who ignores the biblical principles on which you stand. What can you do or say to let this person know that he or she is not honoring the God who holds you both in his hand? What might the consequences be?

"You did not honor the God who holds in his
hand your life and all your ways."

—Daniel 5:23

- 6 -

JUDGE OF THE WHOLE EARTH

Daniel 5:18-31

The news Daniel has for Babylon's King Belshazzar is not good. He reads the words on the wall of the banquet hall: "MENE, MENE, TEKEL, PARSIN" (Dan. 5:25). Mincing no words, Daniel explains that the true God—the ruler of every king on earth—has had enough of Belshazzar's pride and arrogance. The mysterious words announce the end of the king's reign. God will now divide Babylon between the Medes and the Persians.

"You may think you are the Lord of heaven," Daniel says to Belshazzar, "but the fact is that you are merely a public servant in God's world. Your authority is a limited appointment, and you are accountable to God. You exist at the disposal of the God 'who holds in his hand your life and all your ways'"(v. 23).

That very night Belshazzar, king of the Babylonians, was slain, and Darius the Mede took over the kingdom. . . .

—Daniel 5:30

What significance does this have for us? Before you erase this story from your memory as just an interesting old fable, consider how the ancient news about Belshazzar continues to explode with fresh implications before our very eyes. Gorbachev and Yeltsin have fallen, Kaunda is out. Legalized apartheid has been overthrown in South Africa. Presidents and prime ministers come and go, many in disgrace. Governments throughout the world rise and fall so quickly that we cannot even remember most of them.

Justice is required in God's world, on God's terms. Belshazzar learned the truth the hard way, as had Israel's and Judah's rulers years before when God passed judgment on them for their faithlessness. However tragic the experience of God's judgment for those who suffer it, the message is clear. God's commandments for right living and righteous governing in this world will not fail. They will not be contradicted. When justice prevails and God's blessings flow to crown it with honor, God is at work and we should give thanks. With that same attitude of thanksgiving, we should remember that the Creator's precepts also manifest their staying power when the Lord judges human pride and injustice. In the end, evil must give way to the sturdy, never-failing truth and power of the divine covenant.

Kingdoms come and go. God's covenantal purposes will endure forever.

REFLECTING . . .

- Why might we tend more often to recognize God at work when we experience blessings than when we witness the passing of judgment?

- Compare Daniel's position under Belshazzar with that of Joseph under Pharoah (Gen. 40-41). How were their positions and the way God used them similar and yet different?

ACTING . . .

- Read the next edition of your Sunday newspaper or your favorite news magazine and note evidences of justice and injustice. Can you see God's sovereign hand in these situations? Is God calling you to "dare to be a Daniel" in any of these areas?

The Most High God is sovereign over the kingdoms of men and sets over them anyone he wishes.

—Daniel 5:21

- 7 -

FIRE AND AX

Hosea 8; Matthew 3:1-12

You corrupt brood of vipers, pretending to be religious leaders!

With great patience and mercy God sent one prophet after another to call Israel back to the covenant, but the people as a whole persisted in disobedience. The Lord of Israel, the Maker they had forgotten, finally had enough and promised to destroy their palaces and fortified cities (Hos. 8:13-14).

God's destructive blow against Israel and Judah finally fell. The heirs of Abraham, Isaac, and Jacob were driven into exile. Decades later, God allowed a small remnant of Judah to return to the land. And many generations after that, one of their offspring, John the Baptist, began preaching repentance, saying, "the kingdom of heaven is near" (Matt. 3:2). When John met Israel's leaders, including the Pharisees and the Sadducees, he spoke biting words.

"You brood of vipers! Who warned you to flee from the coming wrath? Produce fruit in keeping with repentance. And do not think you can say to yourselves, 'We have Abraham as our father.' I tell you that out of these stones God can raise up children for Abraham. The ax is already at the root of the trees, and every tree that does not produce good fruit will be cut down and thrown into the fire."

—Matthew 3:7-10

Today, the fire of judgment approaches our towns and villages, announcing the arrival of a righteous God. God used Assyria and Babylon for divine purposes—even to judge Israel; God continues to use the nations, for judgment and blessing. The ax of God's condemnation drops to cut off the distorted fantasy we've tried to create for ourselves.

The landlord comes to collect the rent. The master arrives to receive an account of the stewards' work. The King stands to judge the laws and policies made by human subordinates in positions of power. Time has run out.

God has sent his final prophet. Jesus Christ has delivered God's words of judgment and hope.

God's words have everything to do with public justice. God's covenant, now sealed by the blood of Jesus, bears witness to divine justice. The Lord's blessings flow down on obedience. Cataclysmic curses, executed by fire and ax, devour those who persist in disobedience and refuse to repent. God has spoken the climactic word of both judgment and blessing in Jesus Christ. Justice is required. Repent, for the kingdom of heaven is at hand!

REFLECTING . . ..

- Why did Israel persist in injustice despite God's repeated prophetic warnings?

- To what extent is the contemporary church like ancient Israel? What evidence of this similarity do you see in your own church?

ACTING . . .

- Talk with members of your congregation who are doctors, teachers, lawyers, public officials, and business people, and ask them to identify the most prevalent sin that people in their professions should repent of. How can Christians in these professions show fruits of repentance? How can you personally encourage people in these professions to stand for justice?

"Prepare the way for the Lord,
make straight paths for him. "

—Matthew 3:3

- 8 -

CHRISTMAS— INTERLUDE OR MAIN EVENT?

Isaiah 59:1-8

For most of us, Christmas is a long-anticipated vacation break from our main activity of work. The Christmas holiday gives families an early winter breathing space in the school schedule. For members of Congress and Parliament, Christmas and Hanukkah provide the excuse for a long recess.

From a biblical point of view, this is upside-down and backwards. Christmas is not first of all an American or international vacation day; it is the birthday celebration of the Messiah who is at work even now, driving all of history—all calendar days and seasons—toward their proper destiny. The center of life's meaning is not our work or school or legislation, but rather the creating, judging, and saving Lord who sustains all our daily activities.

Israel had been called by God to live among the nations as a faithful testimony to God's love and justice. The chosen people were to order all of their work and rest in ways that would serve as a beacon to people everywhere, as a clear pointer to the God who fulfills covenant promises. When the Israelites lost their grip on this truth, they sank into the mire of ordinary nationhood. And God was outraged.

So the Lord of heaven and earth told Isaiah to tell a dull and sinful Israel that judgment was on its way, a judgment required and promised by the covenant itself.

---

*For your hands are stained with blood, your fingers
with guilt. Your lips have spoken lies, and your
tongue mutters wicked things. No one calls for
justice; no one pleads his case with integrity. They
rely on empty arguments and speak lies; they
conceive trouble and give birth to evil.*

—Isaiah 59:3-4

Israel had continued to celebrate festivals and holidays. Many of the people remembered the exodus from Egypt and offered sacrifices

41

on holy days. Most had kept up some ceremonial practices. But by the time Isaiah arrived on the scene, all of these religious ceremonies and holidays had been domesticated. The children of Israel thought God belonged to them and could be pigeonholed into their busy schedules. They thought they had arrived and quit looking to see where God was still leading them.

Special days and monuments are set aside for a reason. They remind us of God's past actions. The key to such memorials is to understand that they point to the God who continues to march out in front of us and to act in new ways. God cannot be confined in memory, in ceremony, in Christian holidays. Christmas loses its meaning if we think of it only as a reminder of something past and finished.

REFLECTING . . .

• What is it about our lack or weakness of faith that allows us to turn perfectly good habits of worship into patterns that close our hearts to the living God?

• What is it about our habits that encourages us to think we can worship God sincerely on one day and perpetuate injustice the next?

ACTING . . .

• Talk with your family about what it would take to redeem Christmas from the holiday calendar and turn it into the focus for perpetual anticipation of Christ's return. Agree to make at least one change in that direction for your next celebration.

We look for light, but all is darkness;
for brightness, but we walk in deep shadows.

—Isaiah 59:9

- 9 -

LIGHT THAT SHATTERS THE DARKNESS

Isaiah 59:9-21; Matthew 4:12-17

Despite Israel's regular celebration of special holy days, the people actually lived in darkness and confusion. Isaiah said they were groping and stumbling like "men without eyes," like the dead among the strong (Isa. 59:9-10).

The Lord Most High had no intention of allowing Israel to defile the appointed festivals and holidays forever. God would not allow the creational purposes to be destroyed. No, the Almighty would act to confirm the covenant that both undergirds and transcends all earthly calendars and ceremonies. God prepared to sweep down on Israel, breaking through all their tired social patterns and rote traditions that block out God.

The LORD looked and was displeased that there was no justice. He saw that there was no one, he was appalled that there was no one to intercede; so his own arm worked salvation for him, and his own righteousness sustained him. He put on righteousness as his breastplate, and the helmet of salvation on his head; he put on the garments of vengeance and wrapped himself in zeal as in a cloak.

—Isaiah 59:15-17

The surprise comes in the way God chose to accomplish judgment and redemption, for the great light that finally dawns on people living in darkness is Jesus, the quiet, humble child who accommodates himself at first to all of the Jewish holy days.

Yet the incarnate Son of God does not lose himself in the events of the Jewish calendar. Christ's work cannot be remembered or grasped by an annual holiday. Christmas marks the beginning of the end of history, the end of the beginning of all creation. The incarnate one came to bear God's judgment against sin, to suffer death in order to satisfy God's just requirements for the entire creation. The One before whom every knee will bow came first to bow before the Father who sent him.

Jesus comes preaching, "Repent, for the kingdom of heaven is near" (Matt. 4:17). Only by heeding this word from God will anyone be able to see the light that gives hope and leads to true justice. Only by entering into Jesus' response to God's condemnation of Israel will we be able to repent and exit the darkness of sin that inhabits us. Only by watching to see what Jesus does and following him where he goes will it be possible to celebrate Christmas aright.

REFLECTING . . .

- What is the difference between the act of remembering a past event of divine intervention and the act of doing justice? Why does God seem more impressed with the latter than the former?

- Would God be impressed with your congregation's confirmation of the covenant during the Christmas season? Are you shattering the darkness in your community?

ACTING . . .

- Isaiah said God was appalled that there was no one to intercede. Think of an example in a family setting, in a workplace, or in your town where no one interceded when someone should have. Decide what you will do the next time you see such a circumstance.

"The people living in darkness have seen a great light; on those living in the land of the shadow of death a light has dawned."

—Matthew 4:16

- 10 -

PREPARING FOR IMMANUEL

Luke 1:67-80

John the Baptist was sent to prepare the way for the coming Messiah, to trumpet the arrival of Jesus Christ, Immanuel. Before John was born, his father anticipated the truth that would define John's career. Filled with the Holy Spirit, Zechariah prophesied that John would prepare the way for the Messiah.

"And you, my child . . . will go before the Lord to prepare the way for him, to give his people the knowledge of salvation through the forgiveness of their sins, because of the tender mercy of our God, by which the rising sun will come to us from heaven to shine on those living in darkness and in the shadow of death, to guide our feet into the path of peace."

—Luke 1:76-79

Many of the Jews living in the land that had once been under their control were expecting the Messiah to release them from the grip of Rome. They were waiting for God to restore them to independence in the promised land and to free them from oppressors forever. But Zechariah's prophecy anticipated something much greater than Israel's freedom from Rome.

The nation that God came to release from its enemies (v. 71) is the one that he is drawing to the light of Jesus, the nation that will follow him "into the path of peace." This nation will include a remnant of Israel, to be sure, but it will include forgiven sinners from all nations. The lineage of the old Israel will not exhaust the lineage of the new Israel.

This also means that no other nation or state may claim the identity of God's chosen people, as if God came in Christ simply to relocate his throne from Israel to Rome, to Paris or Mexico City, to Berlin or Beijing, to Moscow or Washington, D.C. The great divide of which Zechariah spoke is not between Jews and Gentiles, between East and West, or between North and South. No, the grand drama that John came to announce reveals the divide between the "rising sun" of the Lord Jesus and all the enemies that stand against him. This drama will be played out in every corner of the world, beginning in Jerusalem, but reaching to encompass every nation, every state, and every human heart.

Take hold of the knowledge of salvation that comes through the forgiveness of sins. Welcome the rising sun that dispels darkness everywhere, and rejoice in the light that gives hope to those who now cower under the shadow of death.

In this spirit, let us bind ourselves so closely to God's people everywhere that our sense of solidarity in Christ will lift us above the confines of parochial political ideologies and will free us to serve the one who is redeeming his people and setting all things right before God. With John the Baptist, let us prepare for the Lord's coming with acts of repentance rooted in and aiming for justice.

REFLECTING . . .

- Why did Jesus call John the greatest of the prophets?

- What acts of repentance do you see in Christian circles today that indicate John's message is still being heard? What evidence do you see to the contrary?

ACTING . . .

- Think of a time recently when you have allowed your own social or political ideas and practices to separate you from one or more of God's people. Pray that the Spirit will enable you to repent and reconcile.

"Praise be to the Lord, the God of Israel. . . . He has raised up a horn of salvation for us . . . to enable us to serve him without fear in holiness and righteousness before him all our days."

—Luke 1:68-69, 74-75

- 11 -

WISDOM AND WEARINESS

Ecclesiastes 1:12-18; Matthew 11:25-30

Another new year begins. The months and seasons will cycle around again. Governing bodies will begin their work again. Another United Nations session will open. Fighting and starvation will ravage people in at least half a dozen countries. Everything seems to repeat itself in an endless rhythm, heading nowhere.

The teacher of Ecclesiastes was king of Jerusalem. He devoted himself to study and the search for wisdom. The conclusion he reached after years of reflection was that nothing in human experience makes sense in and of itself; everything is meaningless, a chasing after wind. Moreover, even the process of obtaining wisdom tired him out and produced sadness (Eccl. 1:18).

The royal teacher recognized life's repetitiveness (vv. 4-11), the common fate of death suffered by everyone—high and low, rich and poor (3:18-21)—and the inability of anyone to know or control the future (2:17-23). Using himself as the fixed point from which to view reality, he could only feel despair when he discovered that neither he nor his kingdom was eternal. With exasperation he exclaimed, "What a heavy burden God has laid on men!" (1:13).

What a contrast when Jesus comes on stage. He assumes that God the Father is the fixed point around which all else revolves. Jesus praises the Father who reveals wisdom to delighted children rather than to the wise and learned (Matt. 11:25). Rather than seeing only endless cycles leading to death, Jesus reveals the true direction of history, which moves not in repetitive cycles that produce despair but toward God's sabbath fulfillment.

Instead of complaining about the heaviness of the burden God has laid on earthly rulers, Jesus offers to lift burdens. The very wisdom of God—Jesus Christ, the one who breaks through all of earth's repetitive cycles—takes onto himself the burdens of humanity and replaces them with the gentle yoke of God's wisdom, a wisdom sufficient to lighten even the duty of governors, legislators, presidents, prime ministers, and kings and queens.

---

*"Come to me, all you who are weary and burdened,
and I will give you rest. Take my yoke upon you and
learn from me, for I am gentle and humble in heart,
and you will find rest for your souls. For my yoke is
easy and my burden is light."*

—Matthew 11:28-30

REFLECTING . . .

- What is the most wearisome, repetitive, meaningless part of politics to you? Why do you find it so?

- Who or what motivates you to keep involved in the fight for justice?

ACTING . . .

- Invite someone in your congregation or community who holds a public office or appointment (local, state/province, or national) to speak to an adult education class or fellowship group about the yoke that public responsibility places on one's shoulders. Discuss how being a Christian helps to make the burden lighter. Organize a prayer support group for this public servant.

---

*"What does man gain from all his labor
at which he toils under the sun?"*

—Ecclesiastes 1:3

- 12 -
AN ENIGMATIC LINE OF SUCCESSION

Acts 2:22-41

Miracles and signs attend the birth of a child named Jesus. During his short life he never escapes controversy. Peter and thousands of others begin to follow him. Eventually they become convinced that their rabbi is the Messiah, the heir to David's throne. Their hopes soar.

Yet what an enigma Jesus turns out to be. He is captured and crucified before he comes close to ascending any throne. Yet not long after his burial, Peter is telling the crowds in the streets of Jerusalem that Jesus really is the Messiah.

"God has raised this Jesus to life, and we are all witnesses of the fact. [He is] exalted to the right hand of God. . . . God has made this Jesus, whom you crucified, both Lord and Christ."

—Acts 2:32-33, 36

Sure enough, Peter must be another one of those crazies—a sectarian nut. Or maybe he's just drunk. That's what many in the crowd suspect. But wait—thousands believe Peter, who is not ranting or stumbling over his words. The truth, which becomes evident from the story he tells, is that Peter met the resurrected Jesus. Moreover, Peter does not retreat from the dangerous political implications of that dramatic event.

Jesus had not performed like a typical king or political leader before his death and resurrection, yet he inspired messianic hope in Peter and continues to inspire the same hope in millions of followers today. The living Jesus has ascended David's throne, located at the right hand of God.

"If this is true, what then shall we do? How shall we respond to this king?" These are the very questions the crowd puts to Peter, who responds with what might seem like an unusual admonition: "Repent and be baptized, everyone of you, in the name of Jesus Christ for the forgiveness of your sins" (v. 38). What a strange call to political action. How does repentance help advance Jesus' kingdom?

What an enigma, this "King Jesus." Yet think about it for a moment. Is Jesus any greater an enigma than the best known political leaders of the past 2000 years? How many millions of people have lived and died in the hope that a Napoleon, or a Lenin, or a Hitler would transform the world? At the height of George Bush's modest four-year presidency, right after the collapse of communism, an international magazine pictured him on its cover with the caption "President of the world." How long did that last? Presidents, kings, and dictators come and go.

Only one empire and only one ruler on earth will finally succeed and never fail. The mystery of the incarnation, death, resurrection, and ascension of Jesus illumines with increasing clarity the enigma of all other kingdoms on earth. To live in political truth is to live in the obedience and hope of his kingdom that will outlast and overrule all others.

REFLECTING . . .

- Reflect on the nature of political power, and try to imagine a leader whose kingdom endures forever. What would have to characterize such a government to keep it from becoming boring or oppressive?

- *Merriam Webster's Collegiate Dictionary* (Tenth Edition) defines *enigma* as "something hard to understand or explain, an inscrutable or mysterious person." Compare Jesus' rule with that of some well-known figure such as Abraham Lincoln, Winston Churchill, or Mao Tse-tung. What is enigmatic about each?

ACTING . . .

- Perhaps you have not encountered "dangerous political implications" like Peter did at Pentecost. Even so, what fears have caused you to retreat from introducing the risen Christ to others in your political arena? Commit to telling at least one person about your King Jesus this week.

"God had promised [David] on oath that he would place one of his descendants on his throne."

—Acts 2:30

- 13 -
GOD'S DWELLING PLACE?

Acts 7; 8:1-4

One of the greatest sermons ever preached by the first Christians was Stephen's before the rulers of Israel. By the Spirit of God, Stephen had come to see that Jesus is the Righteous One sent to meet God's requirement of justice.

Stephen's sermon is simply a story—the story of how God has been at work blessing and judging Abraham and his descendants, even to the present day. The story is built upon the underlying questions of how and on what terms God dwells with his chosen people. Did God settle down permanently with Abraham in Canaan? No, but God promised the land to Abraham's descendants. Did God take up residence with Moses in Egypt? No, God came there to lead Israel into the promised land. Did God rest after finally taking Israel into the promised land? No, though the Lord allowed a moveable tabernacle and then a temple to be built as symbols of the divine presence and transcendence.

> *". . . the Most High does not live in houses made by men. As the prophet [Isaiah] says: 'Heaven is my throne, and the earth is my footstool. What kind of house will you build for me? says the Lord. Or where will my resting place be? Has not my hand made all these things?'"*
>
> —Acts 7:48-50

God's "dwelling" with Abraham, Isaac, and Jacob (Israel) always had the character of pointing beyond, pointing ahead. It was more of a "walking beside" than a "sitting down." God was on the move and asked Israel to follow.

Stephen, at the time he relates this story, is struggling with fellow Jews who claim to be God's people yet refuse to acknowledge that the Lord of the law has come. At last, the Righteous One, Jesus of Nazareth, God's Messiah, came to show how God dwells in and rules the earth. Stephen brazenly charges that those who believed they were righteous, the ones who thought God already dwelt with them, had killed Jesus just as their ancestors killed the prophets before him (Acts 7:52).

Before Stephen can say more, his audience explodes in anger. Looking up to heaven, Stephens says, "I see heaven open and the Son of Man standing at the right hand of God" (v. 56). That is too much. The angry crowd drags him outside the city gates and pummels him to death.

Our challenge today is not much different from Stephen's. God calls us to follow the one who has triumphed over death, who judges those who judge us, who is out in front of us and already seated at the right hand of God. God's manner of dwelling with us has been revealed in Jesus, who came to lead, not to stay. The Lord invites us to follow him, even through death, to the promised land of his rule over the whole earth. God will not be confined by any nation.

REFLECTING . . .

- If the earth is the footstool in God's throne room, then what does that say about the location and responsibility of nations like the United States or Canada?

- Compare Stephen's sermon with Hebrews 3-4. Describe the relationship between "dwelling" and "journey" or between "house" and "pilgrimage" found in these two passages.

ACTING . . .

- Peter, Stephen, and members of the early church preached the word wherever God placed them. Identify one place where God is calling you to stand up for Jesus, and spend time in prayer and preparation.

Those who had been scattered
preached the word wherever they went.

—Acts 8:4

- 14 -

THE PASSING OF AN ERA

Isaiah 65:17-25

On October 19, 1987, the second major stock-market crash of the twentieth century symbolized an era of increasing international financial insecurity. At the same moment, the start-up of another American election campaign marked the end of the Reagan era. Both domestically and internationally, both inside and outside politics, Americans were witnessing major historical changes. And still to come, not yet anticipated in 1987, were the even more startling events of 1989—the collapse of communist governments in Eastern Europe and the Soviet Union.

When shocking changes like these take place, most people feel fearful or at least more uncertain about the future. No matter how hard we try, we cannot secure our own lives. Even in stable times, we realize that we cannot pin down or hold on to the present moment. We are by nature propelled into the future and toward an ultimate goal that is beyond our grasp. And in the process, we cannot keep from either dreaming or cringing, from planning or worrying, from hoping or fearing. Thus, when the present seems dark and the future unclear, we often become fearful and insecure.

Isaiah in his day told Israel that the passing of each and every historical era should remind people that the entire human era—all of human history—is destined to pass on. However, history will not simply disappear into a black hole. Instead, this age passes into the hands of the one who has authority to deliver final judgment and final rewards.

The Kingdom of God, says Isaiah, is about to manifest itself in the Lord's triumph over all earthly kingdoms. Isaiah is not writing science fiction. He is speaking about real history, which is about to reach a real culmination.

> *"Behold, I will create new heavens and a new earth. The former things will not be remembered, nor will they come to mind."*
>
> —Isaiah 65:17

The God of justice proclaims that in the Day of the Lord, greedy stock-market speculators will no longer be allowed to ruin the livelihood of others. Financial and commodity markets will no longer crash down on the innocent. Industrial, commercial, and political authorities will be called to account. No longer will God's chosen ones "build houses and others live in them, or plant and others eat. For as the days of a tree, so will be the days of my people; my chosen ones will long enjoy the works of their hands" (v. 22).

The God of justice will cause every injustice to come crashing down in order to pour out the blessings of the covenant on the faithful. The context for assessing every human action, both corporate and personal, is and always will be the blessings and curses of God's trustworthy covenant. Justice is required, and God will deliver, but not simply in condemnation. The Lord will establish his people in peace and security and joy.

REFLECTING . . .

- What are your greatest anxieties today? Which of them are related to political, economic, and social conditions?

- What hope does this passage from Isaiah give you?

ACTING . . .

- Take time to volunteer at a homeless shelter or soup kitchen. Ask some of the people what their greatest anxieties are and how they happened to come to the shelter or kitchen. Share with them the hope expressed in Isaiah 65:17-25. (Be prepared to be part of God's answer to their needs!)

Before they call I will answer;
while they are still speaking I will hear.

—Isaiah 65:24

- 15 -

THE ROOTS OF A TRANSNATIONAL VISION

Isaiah 42:1-9

Christians should not find it difficult to approach civic responsibility from a supra-national point of view—not *anti*-national, but *supra*-national. Serving the God who blesses the rule of Jesus Christ over the entire world, we should humbly accept our civic responsibility as a stewardship before the Lord who rules heaven and earth.

Nevertheless, a prevalent spirit remains in our age that grips American and Canadian Christians as easily as it does nationalists the world over. When it comes to politics we often tend to look at the world from a national-centered perspective—our country, right or wrong, first in line, Number One.

Long before the birth of Jesus, the prophets of ancient Israel told anyone who had ears to hear that the God of Israel does not act on Israel's command. The true God calls all nations, including Israel, to judgment. The Almighty One has raised up a servant to judge the nations and to redeem the Lord's chosen people. God's servant will give water to the thirsty and make the deserts fertile. Idols will be crushed, and God's Messiah will establish justice.

"Here is my servant, whom I uphold, my chosen
one in whom I delight; I will put my Spirit on him
and he will bring justice to the nations. He will not
shout or cry out, or raise his voice in the streets.
A bruised reed he will not break, and a smoldering
wick he will not snuff out. In faithfulness he will
bring forth justice; he will not falter or be
discouraged till he establishes justice on earth.
In his law the islands will put their hope."

—Isaiah 42:1-4

The basis for a truly supra-national or transnational vision of politics is found in the God who did, indeed, make a special covenant with Israel. But that God, says Isaiah, is the one "who created the heavens and stretched them out, who spread out the earth and all that comes out of it, who gives breath to its people, and life to those who walk on it" (Isa. 42:5).

Jesus Christ is, indeed, a son of David, son of Israel. But before that, he is the Son of God, through whom all things were made. The incarnate Son, through death and resurrection, has earned the right to rule and is the only one authorized to call every other authority to account. Christ's chosen ones inherit his kingdom; he is not confined to one of theirs.

Wake up! God's faithful servant, the King of kings, has come and is coming to judge the nations and to redeem his people. Justice is required! God's servant will establish it.

REFLECTING . . .

- Why is Jesus' political authority so difficult to see and understand? Why does it seem so far removed from the other governments we experience?

- Note the number of times the word *justice* is used in Isaiah 42. Based on the things Isaiah praises and condemns, what do you think he means by this term?

ACTING . . .

- Check your thoughts and words over the next several days and note how many times you think and speak as though your country is "Number One" with God. Covenant with one other Christian to break this spirit of confining God.

"I am the LORD; that is my name!"

—Isaiah 42:8

JUSTICE RESTRAINED

It is not to angels that he has subjected the world to come, about which we are speaking. But there is a place where someone has testified:

"What is man that you are mindful of him, the son of man that you care for him? You made him a little lower than the angels; you crowned him with glory and honor and put everything under his feet."

In putting everything under him, God left nothing that is not subject to him. Yet at present we do not see everything subject to him. But we see Jesus, who was made a little lower than the angels, now crowned with glory and honor because he suffered death, so that by the grace of God he might taste death for everyone.

—Hebrews 2:5-9

G od commissioned men and women to govern the earth, but the kind of governance we see around us is not what it ought to be. All is not properly subject to humans because they do not act as faithful stewards in obedience to God. Sinful disobedience distorts the whole of creation and its relation to God.

The penalty for sin is death. If the Judge of all the earth executed the promised penalty for sin immediately and in every instance, no one would live. But without the unfolding of the human generations, governance of the creation under God could not exist. So as the Scriptures explain, for the love of creation the Almighty has been restraining both judgment and sin to allow the creation and human history to unfold.

All have sinned and fall short of the glory of God,
and are justified freely by his grace through the
redemption that came by Christ Jesus. God
presented him as a sacrifice of atonement, through
faith in his blood. He did this to demonstrate his
justice, because in his forbearance he had left the
sins committed beforehand unpunished—
he did it to demonstrate his justice at the present
time, so as to be just and the one who justifies
those who have faith in Jesus.

—Romans 3:23-26

Rainbow Justice

Throughout history God both demonstrates and restrains the ultimate implementation of divine justice. In the time of Noah, sin had become so dense and destructive that God executed a nearly final judgment (Gen. 6-8). Only Noah and his family and the creatures protected in their ark were saved from the flood that wiped out life on earth. Only through Noah did life become possible for future generations. In that sense, Noah foreshadowed Jesus Christ as one through whom God saved sinners from ultimate judgment. God's rainbow covenant with Noah promised restraint of the full impact of divine justice for generations to come. Despite the fact that the generations following Noah would again pollute the earth with unrighteousness, the Lord promised never again to destroy the earth by flood (9:8-17).

God's rainbow covenant not only promised the restraint of judgment against human sinfulness, it also extended new responsibilities to humans as a demonstration of God's justice. The Lord told Noah that the act of taking another human life should be punished by an official act of retribution—the death penalty for a murderer.

Whoever sheds the blood of man,
by man shall his blood be shed; for in
the image of God has God made man.

—Genesis 9:6

The Almighty is restraining final judgment of sinful human beings in order to bring the creation to fulfillment. But in the meantime, the heinous crime of murder and other lesser crimes should not go unpunished. Human sin as well as divine judgment must be restrained in order to make society possible in a sinful world.

One of the consequent blessings of the Lord's patience and restraint is that all human creatures, even those who ignore or reject God, may experience life in God's world. Rain and sunshine fall on the just and the unjust alike. In fact, Jesus told his disciples that they should not attempt to enact God's final judgment by trying to separate the wheat from the tares in the field of this world (Matt. 13:24-30, 36-43). The timing and the actual achievement of the final judgment remain in God's hands.

Human Government and Politics

The political implications of all this are vast. The followers of Jesus must yield to Jesus, the one who holds all authority in heaven and on earth, the one who suffered death for everyone and by means of his death and resurrection gives assurance that justice will be established and creation fulfilled (Matt. 28:18). If Jesus has not yet separated the wheat from the tares, but continues, by the power of the Spirit, to hold back God's judgment and to restrain sin, then his followers must seek to live at peace with all people on earth. Those who claim to follow Jesus should give their lives in service even to their enemies as a demonstration of the Savior's patience and love toward everyone (Rom. 12:17-21). Abiding by God's restraint means that political governance on earth should protect the civil rights of both believers and unbelievers and leave ultimate vengeance in God's hands.

However, we should not misidentify such nondiscriminatory governance as something *secular,* as if political order can be built apart from God on the foundation of human reason and good intentions alone. A political order that offers the same civil rights to all citizens is not a secular state in the sense of being independent of God's grace and justice. Rather, it is a state grounded in Christ's own governance through mercy and restraint; it is government established by God for our good. A state that does not give special privileges to Christians but treats people of all faiths equally is a state that manifests the Lord's patient, merciful governance of the entire creation. That kind of state is the fruit of God's rainbow love, of God's common grace, of God's restraint of final judgment.

You've heard the expression "Carrot and stick." The carrot, a positive reward, entices good behavior; the stick, a threat of punishment, deters or punishes bad behavior.

A public legal system, even as imperfect as ours, offers a means of restraining those who might otherwise seek private revenge. The carrot is the opportunity for offended parties to seek nonviolent redress of grievance through proper channels. The stick is the strong arm of law enforcement that threatens potential offenders with penalties and punishment. The fact that more people do not resort to violence to exercise private vengeance is due, in part, to the fear of punishment. Not everyone can be enticed into good behavior by the carrot of nonviolent legal processes or deterred from bad behavior by the threat of public punishment, but a healthy legal system can go a long way toward restraining the exercise of private vengeance.

Political governance is not the only kind of human governance, of course, and a just state is one that will recognize its own limits in relation to the authority God has given to other kinds of institutions and relationships. As God in Christ through the Holy Spirit holds back the final judgment and restrains sin, human beings of all faiths are allowed to eat and drink, to marry and have children, to study and work, to think and act in this age. God's restraint of both sin and divine justice makes possible the development of all human vocations. Sinful disobedience continues to distort, mislead, and often ruin life, but as long as the Lord's patience endures, there is opportunity for human beings to repent, to turn from their evil ways, and to recognize that life is sustained by God's grace and mercy rather than by human ingenuity.

Living by Faith

By faith, Christians already know that Jesus Christ has been crowned with glory and honor because he tasted death for everyone. Because of Christ, God is holding back final judgment for a time, but the day is coming when the full justice achieved through Jesus Christ will fill the earth. When God's restraining grace in Christ has achieved its purpose, then justice will be established everywhere and in all things. When the time is right, the Judge of all the earth will return.

In the end it will be shown that God has acted justly toward the whole creation. Everything good will reach fulfillment; sin and death will be destroyed. At present, then, we should work for human governments that reflect the Lord's patience, giving evenhanded treatment to every person and punishing crime so that all might live and experience God's grace. Full justice will not be restrained forever. The Ruler of all rulers on earth, the one who suffered God's judgment against sin in order to set everything straight, has been crowned with glory and honor.

Therefore God exalted him to the highest place
and gave him the name that is above every name,
that at the name of Jesus every knee should bow,
in heaven and on earth and under the earth,
and every tongue confess that Jesus Christ is Lord,
to the glory of God the Father.

—Philippians 2:9-11

REFLECTING . . .

- Along with the story of Noah, what other biblical stories illustrate God's gracious restraint of ultimate justice?

- What evidences do you see around you today of sin being restrained? Of God withholding divine judgment, restraining the full execution of divine justice?

- What kinds of responsibility for restraining sin belong to government in contrast to other institutions? How does that reflect God's patience and mercy?

ACTING . . .

- Review the history of the civil rights movement and its impact on your local community or state/province. What role are you willing to take to assure that the civil rights of both believers and unbelievers are protected?

JUSTICE HAPPENING

The crime is committed, the confession is made, community is broken. How will justice be achieved?

Pastor John deVries works as an advocate for restorative justice within the Canadian penal system. During his many years as a prison chaplain, he has seen the ugly side of crime and hardened hearts. He is not naive about crime, yet he asks this question about the present system of justice:

> When people serve time, they are de-socialized. In our modern legal system, professionals remove the offense and the offender from community into the "system." Then, when they finish their sentence, offenders are returned to the community. Prison may punish, but it doesn't make people accountable for their actions. When we practice retribution, who gets healed?

Now deVries is committed to a restorative justice ministry. Explaining the process and goals of the ministry, deVries says:

> If both the victim and offender agree, the judge may send the parties through a restorative process rather than through the court system. With the help of a trained mediator and in the presence of their support groups, the victim and the offender meet face to face in family conference sessions. Restorative justice demands that the offenders recognize and come to terms emotionally with themselves and their crime.

"The New Testament is about God's plan for administering restorative justice," deVries firmly believes. "God's plan is to restore our relationship to himself and to our neighbor. That brings healing."

MEDITATIONS 16-30

- 16 -
RAINBOW JUSTICE
Matthew 5:43-48

"It's not right. There ought to be a law against that." You've probably heard this said before. I've said it myself. But who should make what kind of law against what kind of wrongdoing?

In the deepest sense of the word *law,* God already has a law against every kind of evil. He commands us to do right, to love our neighbors, to do justice. Still, in human terms, how should we promote good and punish evil? Should the state pass laws to punish parents who do not brush their children's teeth every day? Should church authorities enforce penalties against parishioners who do not keep their yards clean?

These may sound like silly questions, but they're not. These questions take us back to God's will for creation. God gave human beings many different kinds of responsibility, different kinds of law-making authority. Engineers building bridges have a different kind of responsibility than parents rearing children. Political authorities should make different kinds of laws than church officials or school administrators make.

But there's something more than rules to the Creator's love for the world. For some mysterious, long-suffering reason, God decided a long time ago to make the rainbow a sign of divine mercy for every creature. It's not that the Righteous One gave up on lawfulness or quit caring about what is good. Rather, the Lord made room in a sinful world for repentance, forgiveness, restoration, reconciliation.

The rainbow anticipated the good act of redemption through Jesus Christ. When Jesus came, God made it clear beyond doubt that doing what is right requires the treatment of all our neighbors the way God treats them. That is rainbow justice, and it now colors and reinforces God's original creation purposes.

"But I tell you: Love your enemies and pray for those who persecute you, that you may be sons of your Father in heaven. He causes his sun to rise on the evil and the good, and sends rain on the righteous and the unrighteous."

—Matthew 5:44-45

Rainbow justice says that human political authorities do not hold
God's responsibility for final judgment in their hands. Rainbow
justice makes room for people to fulfill the different kinds of responsibility they have in homes, at work, in church, and in government
while giving them time to turn from doing evil and begin doing what
is right. Rainbow justice is a revelation of God's will in Jesus Christ,
and there can be no law against that.

REFLECTING . . .

• What kinds of laws do you think government should pass? What
  kinds of laws belong to families, churches, schools, and businesses?
  Why?

• What examples can you think of that indicate government is
  making laws that belong to families, churches, schools, and
  businesses?

ACTING . . .

• The next time you see a rainbow, count the colors you see and
  then think of all the colors of God's love that it represents: patience, restraint of righteous indignation, preservation of creatures,
  warning to repent, redeeming grace. . . . How are you reflecting
  these colors in your relationships with others?

*"Be perfect, therefore, as your
heavenly Father is perfect."*

—Matthew 5:48

- 17 -

TEMPTING, ISN'T IT?

Luke 4:5-8; 11:4

In August and September of 1988, the nearly 2000-year-old Jesus received almost as much attention from the media (including a *Time* magazine cover story) as did presidential candidates George Bush and Michael Dukakis. While the candidates' managers were trying to make them look like gods to get our votes, Martin Scorsese, in *The Last Temptation of Christ,* was trying to make Jesus look purely human so we would no longer feel guilty for having rejected his divine claims and mandates. Scorsese's movie was a cover-up, an attempt to help us hide from the truth that, in our weakness, we succumb to the temptation of wanting to be God.

The greatest and perhaps the last temptation to take control of human beings is the modern illusion that we may be able to gain sole ownership and complete mastery of this planet and its surrounding heavens. The temptation is so powerful that nothing has been able to block it. Space shuttle disasters, greenhouse effects, failed dictatorships, plagues and diseases, wars and rumors of wars—nothing has brought more than a small percentage of people to their knees to pray.

"'Forgive us our sins. . . .
And lead us not into temptation.'"

—Luke 11:4

Whether by means of science and technology or through politics and art, moderns seem driven by the Faustian desire to master the world in order to be able to dictate and control the terms of life. "If God is not dead," they seem to be saying, "he ought to be."

In contrast to Jesus, who resisted the devil's temptation to take control of all the kingdoms of this world, we have long since perfected the art of yielding to this temptation while hiding from the truth that we have become enslaved to a devilish god. Chained to an illusion, we pridefully imagine that we are, or soon will be, in full control.

This is one reason why so much of our contemporary politics is more like theater than reality. Politicians know we want everything, including instant solutions to all problems, so they paint a rosy picture of the world they promise to help us achieve. We, in turn, want to hear their grand promises rather than the balanced truth about reality, so we demand ever more grandiose promises. Of course, reality keeps marching on, with its debt burdens, its drop-out rates, and its ecological degradations. But we remain caught in the snare of temptation, unable and unwilling to bow in repentance before the only One who can deliver us.

Yet, despite our denial of God, we cannot escape from Jesus. No one produces movies on the last temptation of Caesar or Napoleon, of St. Augustine or Martin Luther. The Jesus who bowed before his Father in heaven rather than yield to the devil's temptation, the Jesus who taught us to pray that we not be led into temptation—this Jesus lives and rules and calls us to turn from the temptation of wanting to be God. Only this Jesus can liberate us from slavery to theatrical politics and from the illusory dream of independent mastery over the world.

REFLECTING . . .

- How has "theatrical politics" impacted you personally? What grandiose promises have left unsolved problems in your community?

- In what areas of your life do you face the temptation of wanting to be God? Which are the hardest to resist? Why?

ACTING . . .

- Consider how you might tackle one of the unsolved problems in your community. You may want to make this an ongoing project during the duration of this study on justice. Perhaps a small group or an entire church or community could become involved in a long-term solution.

"Worship the Lord your God and serve him only."

—Luke 4:8

- 18 -

A LITTLE, WITH RIGHTEOUSNESS

Proverbs 16:8-9; Matthew 5:6, 25:19-30

"Better a little with righteousness than much gain with injustice"
(Prov. 16:8). I doubt it. Better for whom? Why? Surely this can't be
true all the time and in every circumstance. A little doesn't go as far as
it used to; more good can be done if you have more. After all, Robin
Hood was a "good guy," wasn't he?

With so much injustice in our world today, shouldn't Christians
welcome a Robin Hood who does a little injustice in order to promote
a far greater good? A "little" with righteousness doesn't amount to
much for the unemployed person who is trying to stay alive in the
streets today. Shouldn't we forgive that person's minor thefts, recognizing the odds he or she faces?

The marketplace is a dog-eat-dog world, and a corporation can hire
more people and produce more goods if it stays on top—even if that
takes a little injustice. Isn't "much gain" better sometimes? Police can
catch more criminals if they use a few unlawful techniques from time
to time; don't we prefer that they "gain" more crooks rather than
only a few?

Clearly this proverb was not devised by human ingenuity. It arises
from a different point of view—from a divine perspective on life. In
fact, the very next proverb gives it away:

"In his heart a man plans his course, but the LORD determines his
steps" (v. 9).

If, in the final analysis, the Lord determines our steps, then it's
divine wisdom that finally matters. And from God's point of view,
what does all of our "gain" amount to anyway? Very little! One might
gain the whole world but lose one's soul. A little, even very little, if it
comes from an obedient response to God, can represent a David
against Goliath or trumpets against the walls of Jericho. What matters
to the Lord is not the "little" or the "much," but whether it is "with
righteousness" or "with injustice."

Jesus illustrated these proverbs when he told the parable of the
talents (Matt. 25:19-30). Biblical revelation about life is always
oriented to the coming of God's kingdom in its fullness. God intends
to fulfill more than our present needs. That's why righteousness
counts for more than immediate satisfaction.

———————

"Well done, good and faithful servant! You have
been faithful with a few things; I will put you in
charge of many things. Come and share your
master's happiness!"

—Mathew 25:21

———————

So then, what attitude will prevail in our daily lives? Will right-eousness or self-satisfaction shape our dealings with our neighbors? What will you and I demand of our candidates for public office? Will we continue to buy into the standard practice of interest-group politics, disregarding the minor—even some major—injustices as long as our interest group gets what it wants? Or will we persist in following the path of justice and righteousness even if it brings us only a little in the short term?

REFLECTING . . .

- If you have little, how do you cope while seeing so many around you with so much? If you have much, how do you cope while seeing so many around you with so little?

- Why can we humans be so quick to figure out how to cut corners or rationalize an injustice, yet so slow to figure out and do what justice demands?

ACTING . . .

- Get acquainted with one family in your church or community who is experiencing "little." Perhaps a single parent with preschoolers, an unemployed or disabled parent with teenagers, or an elderly person caring for a spouse with Alzheimer's just needs a word of encouragement, a helping hand. Your "little" won't fix their problems, but you can share your Master's happiness.

———————

"Blessed are those who hunger and thirst for
righteousness, for they will be filled."

—Matthew 5:6

———————

- 19 -

JESUS AND NEOPAGANISM

Acts 4:1-31

Vanity Fair magazine calls it "hilarious . . . a full frontal assault on the New Testament." "It" happens to be the novel *Live From Golgotha*—the gospel according to Gore Vidal, one of today's most articulate neopagans.

The attacks on Jesus continue to mount. Vidal, like Nietzsche before him, derides Jesus for his unmanly passivity. But at the same time, Vidal charges Christians with having carried through an imperial assault on everything good in life. He seems to be saying that if only people could forget Jesus, they could get on with the pursuit of real happiness.

Who is this Jesus who appears to be such a threat to happiness? He and his earliest followers emerged from utter weakness. Jesus never gained power in Israel. He did not even try to drive out the Roman authorities from the Jewish region. His most ardent followers, like Peter and John, had no access to Random House (Vidal's publisher) or the nightly news. To win a following, the disciples did "awful" things like healing crippled people and giving them hope for eternity. They preached from prison where they were locked up for the horrible crime of exciting people's imaginations.

When Jesus' followers were not locked up in prison, they spent time mapping out plans for "revenge" against the authorities by—I have to say it, no matter how embarrassing—by praying! They prayed to the sovereign Lord who "made the heaven and the earth and the sea, and everything in them" (Acts 4:24), and asked him to enable them "to speak your word with great boldness. Stretch out your hand," they pleaded, "to heal and perform miraculous signs and wonders through the name of your holy servant Jesus" (vv. 29-30).

For Gore Vidal, there is no sin, no repentance, no forgiveness in this damn-God world. But strange, isn't it, that for all his bravado Vidal cannot shake Jesus. From his viewpoint, he had better stay on the attack because a few million people out there continue the dangerous practice of prayer that they learned from Peter and John. And the Spirit still gives boldness.

After they prayed, the place where they were meeting
was shaken. And they were all filled with the Holy
Spirit and spoke the word of God boldly.

—Acts 4:31

In the final analysis, it's not Christian faith that threatens happiness in this world. Christians don't display their greatest strength when they act like pagans and compete by using the tools of cynicism, mockery, and violence. With neopagan revivals continuing all around us, we had better draw from our roots—from the weakness of prayer and good deeds.

REFLECTING . . .

- In what ways can you see God's restraint of justice at work, allowing Gore Vidal and neopaganism to flourish?

- What examples do you see in your community of the "weakness" of prayer and good deeds displaying great strength?

ACTING . . .

- Take time this week to pray for God to change the heart of someone near you who mocks Christianity and to show you how you might be of service to that person.

"There is no other name under heaven
given to men by which we must be saved."

—Acts 4:12

- 20 -

THE QUIET, PATIENT PUSH FOR JUSTICE

Isaiah 42:1-4; Matthew 12:15-21

There is a time for everything under the sun, including noise and impatience. But when it comes to the urgency of establishing justice, God is not always loud or rushed. Not that God is unconcerned about injustice. It's simply that justice is a giant thing with the Almighty, and it takes time to achieve it. The Lord will have it no other way.

Indeed, God sticks by the promise to do justice to all creation, giving humans time, in their generations, to be born, to live, and to bear responsibility. God does not fail to do justice, but divine patience with sinful creatures does make room for human disobedience.

On occasion, the Lord has responded to human injustice with devastating speed and fearfully loud noises. The Righteous One once flooded the earth in judgment; the Judge of all nations used Moses to lead a noisy and destructive exodus from Egypt; the Liberator allowed Joshua and his company to knock down the walls of Jericho with trumpet blasts. Yet none of these deeds completed God's just purposes once and for all.

Then one day God gave Isaiah a vision of a quiet servant who would endure quietly, patiently, and without discouragement until justice was established on earth. Centuries later, the gospel writer Matthew explained that when the Pharisees had finally had enough of Jesus and were plotting to kill him, Jesus decided to hide from them. People kept following him, and Jesus kept healing their sick, but he had no interest in shouting down the Pharisees or trying to win a quick argument with them. So Jesus warned those who followed him "not to tell who he was" (Matt. 12:16).

Why did Jesus do this? According to Matthew, it was because Jesus is the very servant anticipated by Isaiah. Jesus is the one who will endure quietly, patiently, without breaking down or crying out, "till he leads justice to victory" (v. 20). Quoting Isaiah, Matthew says that in the name of Jesus "the nations will put their hope" (v. 21).

---

*"He will bring justice to the nations. He will not
shout or cry out, or raise his voice in the streets.
A bruised reed he will not break, and a
smoldering wick he will not snuff out. In
faithfulness he will bring forth justice."*

—Isaiah 42:1-3

There is no simple moral to this story. Jesus did not always hide or remain quiet. He did not always insist on keeping his identity a secret. He did not tell his followers never to protest injustice in the streets. But the main point is this: God's chosen servant will endure until he has finally established justice. The servant is Jesus, the patient one who proclaims justice to the nations. Jesus will not fail. Our urgency need not be anxious. Our quest for justice should grow from patience but never quit.

REFLECTING . . .

- How does God's patience in allowing rebellious creatures to exercise responsibility in families, at work, and in government reveal God's justice to creation?

- Compare the different kinds of "long-range development" involved in rearing children, in completing a major research project in an industry or at a university, and in changing a public law. How does an understanding of a long-range process or project help us understand God's patience in establishing justice?

ACTING . . .

- Think of a situation where you've been tempted to quit or have actually given up a fight for justice. Commit today to take one small action that will rekindle a quiet, patient commitment to this cause.

---

*"He will not falter or be discouraged till he
establishes justice on earth."*

—Isaiah 42:4

- 21 -

IN THE SIGHT OF ALL PEOPLE

Luke 2:21-40

Unless one is cursing, mentioning the name of Jesus in public usually causes some embarrassment—except perhaps on Christmas Day when even National Public Radio broadcasts carols and oratorios that tell the whole world that Jesus is King and Lord and Savior. In the eyes of most people, after all, Jesus is a private god who belongs to a particular religious group, not to everyone. To speak of Jesus in the presence of a wider public, which does not revere him, requires an explanation or produces embarrassment.

According to the historical account, the embarrassment caused by Jesus arises not because he is a private god who is sometimes mistakenly referred to as a public figure by his cultic followers. Rather, the awkward problem with Jesus is precisely that he is the public God-man who claims lordship over everything and everyone on earth, including those who do not acknowledge him.

Eight days after Jesus was born, before he could personally claim anything about himself, his parents took him to be circumcised as required by the law of Israel. No sooner had they entered the temple grounds then an old prophet came over and took the baby in his arms. God had revealed ahead of time to Simeon that this Jesus was "the Lord's Christ" (Luke 2:26), the Messiah promised long ago. He was born not just to confirm Israel's glory, but to be "a light for revelation to the Gentiles" (v. 32).

"Sovereign Lord, as you have promised, you now dismiss your servant in peace. For my eyes have seen your salvation, which you have prepared in the sight of all people, a light for revelation to the Gentiles and for glory to your people Israel."

—Luke 2:29-32

If, in contrast to this testimony, it is correct to treat Jesus as a private, sectarian god, then we need to be honest and confess that Matthew, Simeon, John, Paul, and, yes, even Jesus, were liars, deranged cultists, lunatics. For their testimony was that Jesus entered the world as God's revelation "in the sight of all people" as the Lord's Christ.

Jesus is either King over all nations or a fraud. Jesus is either the only Lord with the right to lay claim to total authority on earth or a man whose followers are foolishly and dangerously blind. The fact that his gracious lordship makes room in the public square for those who refuse to acknowledge him does not mean that Jesus has accepted a diminished, private status. It proves only that the power of his mercy, patience, and love now rule the day until the time of his even more embarrassing visitation in the future.

REFLECTING . . .

- What is the difference between embarrassment one may feel when making a public claim about Jesus and embarrassment one may feel when someone makes such a claim in an offensive way or in a way that easily confirms the unbeliever's misconception of Jesus?

- Think about the difference between a private or sectarian god who belongs only to one group and the public Lord Jesus, who is Sovereign over all but acknowledged only by some people. What consequences should this have for the way we worship, work, and exercise our civic responsibilities?

ACTING . . .

- Deliberately subject yourself to embarrassment by taking a stand on an issue that requires you to make a public claim about Jesus, such as screening pornography on computers in your local public library, protesting local zoning laws that would keep out those who want to minister to drug addicts, and so on.

And the child grew and became strong; he was filled with wisdom, and the grace of God was upon him.

—Luke 2:40

- 22 -

VENGEANCE IS MINE

Deuteronomy 32:35-36; 2 Kings 6:8-23; Luke 6:27-28

Salim Munayer, an Arab Christian who is a citizen of Israel, spoke in Washington some years before the 1993 Arab-Israeli peace agreement. His burden was the deadly cycle of vengeful retaliation in the Middle East where an act of violence is often met with a retaliatory act of equal or greater violence. The mentality behind this cycle goes back countless generations.

One of the greatest contributions Christians can make, Mr. Munayer said, is to show how the cycle of retaliatory violence can be broken when we let God work.

In his parting song before his death, Moses reminded the children of Israel to leave ultimate judgment and vengeance in God's hands. In spite of their ongoing rebellion, God promised to have "compassion on his servants" (Deut. 32:36).

"It is mine to avenge; I will repay."

—Deuteronomy 32:35

One of the best illustrations of how human restraint, reflecting God's own restraint, can break the cycle of violence is presented in the story about Elisha and the Arameans in 2 Kings 6. The king of Aram keeps trying to engage Israel in battle, but God gives Elisha advance warning each time so that Israel's armies can stay out of the way.

Eventually the Aramean king discovers that the prophet Elisha is in Dothan and sends a strong force to surround the city. Elisha's servant is frightened, but Elisha asks the Lord to let his servant see the far greater number of surrounding horses and chariots God has provided. Then God blinds the oncoming Arameans so that Elisha can lead them into Samaria where Israel's king is positioned. When God opens their eyes, they stand face to face with Israel's forces.

Israel's king then asks Elisha a very natural question: "Shall I kill them, my father? Shall I kill them?" (v. 21).

Elisha answers, "Do not kill them." Instead, "'set food and water before them so that they may eat and drink and then go back to their master.' So he prepared a great feast for them, and after they had finished eating and drinking, he sent them away, and they returned to their master" (vv. 22-23).

What was the outcome of this seemingly foolish act of feeding one's enemies? The text concludes with these words: "So the bands from Aram stopped raiding Israel's territory" (v. 23).

"You see," Salim Munayer explained that day in Washington, "this is an important lesson about how to break the cycle of violence by avoiding retaliation."

Learning to become a peacemaker, to turn the other cheek, to return good for evil, to break the cycle of violence, is not an innovation for weaklings and soft-hearted pacifists. We are all sinners deserving judgment; God's restraining grace makes it possible for life to continue. Those who have experienced that grace should also exercise it.

REFLECTING . . .

- Why does turning the other cheek or feeding one's enemies seem to be such a mistaken thing to do? Why does it not feel like the natural thing to do?

- In his second inaugural address, Abraham Lincoln reverently spoke of "the justice and goodness of God." Knowing what history has told us about the Civil War, how was—and is—this reverence a call for humans to humble themselves before God about their ability to know and to do justice?

ACTING . . .

- Hard as it may be to admit, name one enemy you have. Commit to pray for that person for one month, and ask for God's grace to "feed" this person in some concrete way.

> "Love your enemies, do good to those
> who hate you, bless those who curse you,
> pray for those who mistreat you."
>
> —Luke 6:27-28

- 23 -

GOD'S REVELATION IN HISTORY

Matthew 24:1-51; Romans 1:14-25; 2:1-11

Is America God's chosen nation for this era? Is the state of Israel a fulfillment of divine prophecy? Was the Soviet Union the evil empire that should have been identified as the anti-Christ? These and many similar questions are asked of me regularly by those who want to know how to discern God's will, God's revelation, in history. What should we look for when we search for God's will here and now?

Even the most specific prophetic passages in the Bible, including Matthew 24, where Jesus himself is speaking, contain much mystery. That mystery is related to the fact that God is directing all of history, not just particular events and interventions in history. All of history reveals God. Moreover, God's will for this world reveals itself in a manner that does not allow us to stand above God or outside history as spectators. No one except the Father knows the day or the hour when heaven and earth will pass away (Matt. 24:35-36). The responsibility of the believer is not to speculate about the mystery but to be faithful in obeying the open commands of the Master (vv. 45-51).

The Scriptures are clear about several things that help answer the questions above. First, God's revelation in history is always a revelation of both blessing and cursing, both redemption and judgment (vv. 45-51). No state or nation or anything else represents God's will or revelation simply by the fact of its existence. God calls every person and institution to act in obedience to divine commands, and God's will is revealed both in judgment against disobedience and in blessing upon obedience. This was as true for ancient Israel as it is for us today.

Second, God's blessings and curses touch all human beings everywhere. The antithesis between righteousness and unrighteousness cannot be located in camps of "good guys" and "bad guys" in history, between democracy and communism, or between America and its enemies, or between the state of Israel and its opponents (Rom. 1:14-25; 2:1-11).

The question for us is not whether we can locate a divinely chosen state or identify some other unambiguous revelation of God's mysterious will. Rather, the question is this: How can we and our governments act responsibly and with humility so that divine blessings rather than curses will be our lot? God's revelation everywhere and at all times both illumines our creational responsibilities and directs us toward the final revelation of the Son of Man. We need not fathom the full mystery of God's will to know how to respond to God's revelation in history. Rather, we need to be doing God's work.

---

*"Who then is the faithful and wise servant, whom
the master has put in charge of the servants in his
household to give them their food at the proper time?
It will be good for that servant whose master finds
him doing so when he returns."*

—Matthew 24:45-46

REFLECTING . . .

- What art or insight does a servant need in order to give members of a household their food at the proper time? How does this picture the work God wants you to do?

- Reflect on these words from Abraham Lincoln's second Inaugural address (1865): "Both [North and South] read the same Bible, and pray to the same God; and each invokes his aid against the other. . . . The prayers of both could not be answered; that of neither has been answered fully." When have you experienced a similar situation?

ACTING . . .

- Identify a public servant you can serve this week, particularly someone with whom you haven't always seen eye-to-eye. Drop a note, make a phone call, or pray for that person to encourage him or her to fill that office wisely.

---

*"Nation will rise against nation
and kingdom against kingdom."*

—Matthew 24:7

- 24 -

BLASPHEMY DESERVES DEATH

John 10:22-42; Colossians 3:1-17; 4:16

"Blasphemy deserves death!" were the words of the Ayatollah Khomeini. Salman Rushdie should die because he blasphemed God in his fictional book, *The Satanic Verses*. Islamic law as interpreted by Khomeini is not the only place where blasphemy is condemned. The biblical Torah condemns blasphemy and treats it as a capital offense. The Jews picked up stones to kill Jesus for "blasphemy, because you, a mere man, claim to be God" (John 10:33). Paul and the other apostles of Christ also wrote to warn that the "wrath of God is coming" because of evil deeds including "malice, slander (blasphemy), and filthy language from your lips" (Col. 3:6-8).

Yet who should enforce the death penalty against blasphemers, and when should it be done? Khomeini, along with some Jews and Christians, says that blasphemy deserves the death penalty today at the hands of political authorities properly constituted under divine law. Secularists, on the other hand, say that blasphemy should never be punished because free speech and a free press should be protected in an open society. Their highest goal is human freedom.

Christians, I believe, should take a different stance. Unlike the secularists, Christians should identify blasphemy for what it is: an outrageous sin by human beings against their Maker, an expression of foolishness and bondage on the part of those who refuse to recognize that the wrath of God will be poured out against such ungodliness.

But at the same time, Christians believe that only one man, Jesus Christ, is qualified to pass final judgment against such sin. Jesus did not ask his disciples to follow a path of searching to destroy blasphemers. In fact, the resurrected Jesus actually called Paul away from such a life when he met Paul on the road to Damascus.

Jesus gave Paul and the other apostles different marching orders. Don't try to play God! Because God is merciful and because humans are so fallible, leave capital punishment against blasphemy in the hands of Jesus Christ who "is seated at the right hand of God" (Col. 3:1). We, like Paul, are called to restraint.

Clothe yourselves with compassion, kindness, humility, gentleness and patience. Bear with each other and forgive whatever grievances you may have

against one another. Forgive as the Lord forgave you.
And over all these virtues put on love, which binds
them all together in perfect unity.

—Colossians 3:12-14

Khomeini is correct that blasphemy deserves death. The secularists are correct that free speech should be protected. Christians should identify blasphemy as foul speech but should leave its final judgment in God's hands. Yet our support for an open society is grounded in God's mercy, not in human freedom. Government should protect free speech, but we should use our tongues to warn blasphemers that the wrath of God is coming.

REFLECTING . . .

- What accounts for the fact that God ordained capital punishment against blasphemy in Israel but restrained the exercise of that penalty in New Testament teaching?

- How can Christians warn against blasphemy on television and in the movies while still expecting government to protect freedom of speech?

ACTING . . .

- If your church is in or near a major city, invite a Muslim authority to come to an adult education class to explain Islamic law and punishment against sins like blasphemy. (Or research this topic at your local library or on the Internet.) Compare Islamic practices with Old and New Covenant teaching, and discuss the implications for the government of an open and pluralistic society.

Let the word of Christ dwell in you richly as you
teach and admonish one another with all wisdom.

—Colossians 4:16

- 25 -

THE MODEST PATIENCE OF THE KING

Luke 24:13-53

One of the great political tensions that has endured for 2000 years arises from the conviction that Christians owe their allegiance to Jesus Christ, the King who claims authority over all other rulers. The tension is complex and powerful.

For one thing, Jesus has not been sighted on the earthly political scene for a long time. For another, his announced supremacy has frequently driven his followers in opposite directions. Some have become convinced that his monarchy is purely other-worldly, so it has little or nothing to do with earthly politics. Others have been so strongly convinced of the immediate relevance of Christ's lordship that they have tried to make governments conform to the terms of Christ's completed kingdom. Neither of these approaches seems right on biblical terms.

The post-resurrection walk that Jesus took with two disciples on the road to Emmaus is extremely revealing in this regard. Jesus is alive from the dead. He has triumphed over sin and the grave. The basis for his claim to universal kingship has been established. But the time is not yet ripe for the final revelation of his rule. Jesus determines to show himself to his followers and to demonstrate the reality of his resurrection. But he does it in a way that restores and empowers his followers to complete their own life callings, not in a way that cuts off or dismisses their responsibilities on earth. Jesus joins two follow-ers walking to Emmaus and begins quietly to explain the meaning of history, including the necessity of the sacrificial death of the one who has become the triumphant Lord.

"Did not the Christ have to suffer these things and then enter his glory?" And beginning with Moses and all the Prophets, he explained to them what was said in all the Scriptures concerning himself.

—Luke 24:26-27

Jesus does not walk around shouting to the public, "Listen, every-one! I am the King of kings. I have done it. Come and join my

crusade until we have forced our way into control of every government on earth." Rather, he remains almost hidden from view in order
to help the disciples see for themselves how they will have to interpret the public record. Future generations of humankind must still be
born. The message of repentance and forgiveness of sins must be
taken to the four corners of the earth before the full extent of Christ's
kingdom can be revealed (Luke 24:45-49). The followers of Christ
may have centuries of work yet to do before Christ's kingdom can be
fully unveiled.

When does it dawn on the two disciples that they have been
walking and talking with the risen Lord Jesus? It happens when Jesus
sits down with them, breaks the bread, and gives thanks to God. The
King of kings first takes time to give the bread of life to his servants.
His aim is to empower them to serve, so they can learn patience in
doing justice, until the time is full for everyone.

REFLECTING . . .

- Why did Jesus want the disciples to discover the truth about
  himself through Scriptural reasoning, when he simply could have
  told them who he was?

- Make a list of the human characteristics that Jesus affirms and
  empowers in this story. Which ones seem most important for the
  way we conduct ourselves in the civic life of the public square?

ACTING . . .

- If you don't already belong to such a group, join or organize a
  group of people with whom you can break bread and open the
  Scriptures. Let the word of God call you to work that still needs to
  be done before Christ's kingdom comes in fullness.

---

*"Were not our hearts burning within us
while he talked with us on the road and
opened the Scriptures to us?"*

—Luke 24:32

- 26 -

LAND, FAITH, AND JUSTICE

Leviticus 25:39-46; Matthew 28:16-20

Certain events taking place on the world stage reveal something quite fascinating. Israel and the Palestinians continue to engage in a process which, if successful, will lead Israel to recognize that Palestinians have a right to some kind of self-rule in a separate territory of their own. It will also bring Palestinian recognition that Jews have distinctive rights of citizenship in a state of their own. A few thousand miles to the south, the people of multiracial South Africa have overturned racial apartheid (separate lands for separate races) in order to gain a single territorial government that will represent all racial groups.

Both of these movements—seemingly in opposite directions—are interpreted as progress by most of the world's leaders. But this forces the question: What constitutes a just state with respect to allocating land to different peoples? Why does it appear acceptable to allocate separate lands and states to separate religious and ethnic groups in the Middle East but completely wrong to do the same in South Africa or North America?

Leviticus 25 speaks of God's demands for justice in the land that Israel was about to receive as a gift from God. At that time and in that place God insisted that no child of Jacob should ever hold a brother or sister in slavery, but God permitted Israelites to buy and sell slaves from other nations. The land was for Israel in particular, and non-Israelites were not always to be treated equally.

---

*"Because the Israelites are my servants,
whom I brought out of Egypt, they must not
be sold as slaves. . . . Your male and female
slaves are to come from the nations around you;
from them you may buy slaves."*

—Leviticus 25:42, 44

This and many other parts of God's covenant with Israel help to explain some contemporary Jewish thinking about the state of Israel, although most Jews would reject slavery and would consider the

United States or Canada unjust if it gave special privileges to Christians or to a particular ethnic group in discrimination against Jews. (The Afrikaners who supported apartheid in South Africa also appropriated for themselves certain Old Testament ideas about God's chosen people entering a new promised land.)

Christians should argue on the basis of passages such as Matthew 28:16-18 that God's authority over the nations as revealed finally in Jesus Christ is so universal that no ethnic or religious group may lay claim, with divine sanction, to special privileges within an earthly state. Given human hard-heartedness, a degree of territorial separation among peoples may be better than perpetual civil war; that's why it's certainly just for the Palestinians to have their own state if Jews and other Arabs are going to have theirs. But ultimately, the Christian argument for equal, non-discriminatory treatment of all citizens within any territorial state, regardless of ethnic and religious identity, grows from the belief that the true God is not a territorial God—unless, of course, one understands that territory to be the whole earth.

REFLECTING . . .

- Why did Jesus claim authority over all the earth but not displace other earthly rulers?

- Use a concordance to find out what slavery meant at the time of Israel's exodus from Egypt and its entrance into the promised land. What are the differences between ancient slavery and the kind that characterized the United States until the Civil War? What are the biblical grounds for arguing that neither is just today?

ACTING . . .

- Examine your "corner" of God's earth—your church, your community—for attitudes and actions that discriminate against ethnic or religious groups. What are you willing to do to break down these "territorial" boundaries?

---

*"All authority in heaven
and on earth has been given to me."*

—Matthew 28:18

- 27 -

IF CHRIST HAS NOT BEEN RAISED

1 Corinthians 15:1-19

Frequently someone will ask me why there is any need for a distinctively Christian political effort. Why shouldn't Christians simply continue to join political coalitions on a common, rational basis with others? I respond by saying that Christians should always work longer and harder than everyone else to cooperate with every group of citizens to strengthen the public trust. But in order to do this, they have to stand firm and build on the deepest foundation they have— the lordship of Jesus Christ who claims their ultimate allegiance as well as authority over all earthly authorities.

The point of a distinctively Christian approach to politics is not that Christians bring something to politics that is unrelated to the common life of everyone. No, sin is everywhere, and the forgiveness of sin is not a private possession of some sect, unrelated to the rationality and sociability that all humans share as creatures of God. Christ's death and resurrection deal with sins. What is it that human beings confront today in public life? Civil wars, revolutions, greed, hatred, and countless unresolvable injustices of every kind abound. Without forgiveness we are dead in sin; justice, among other things, is frustrated.

God's raising of Christ from the dead gives assurance that the forgiveness of sin is real. The gospel calls everyone to repentance. Repentance from sin, including repentance from public injustices that we commit against our neighbors, makes genuine politics possible. Those who accept God's forgiveness of sin in Christ can begin living with a new frame of mind and an openness to both God's requirement of justice and God's restraint of justice.

Christ died for our sins according to the Scriptures,
. . . he was buried, . . . he was raised on the
third day according to the Scriptures. And if
Christ has not been raised, our preaching is
useless and so is your faith.

—1 Corinthians 15:3-4, 14

Political life is a human affair. Human sinfulness touches politics. Thus, repentance from public injustice is crucial if there is to be any hope for justice in the governing of civic life. But repentance is not possible without forgiveness. The good news of the gospel is that God forgives sins through Christ's sacrificial death. If Christ is still dead, then we have no hope for life based on forgiveness because we are still dead in our sins.

All of life in this world hangs on the resurrection of Christ that makes possible the forgiveness of sins. Christians cannot attempt to make a healthy contribution to political life if they do not build together on the foundation of that confession. The shame is that we know very little of what the forgiveness of sin means for politics, and many of us seem to be in no hurry to find out what it means. O Lord, forgive us our sins.

REFLECTING . . .

- Reflect on the relationship between Christ's resurrection from the dead and God's common grace to all people on earth through government.

- Do you agree that Christians "seem to be in no hurry to find out" what forgiveness means? What evidence can you give to support or contradict this assessment?

ACTING . . .

- Conduct an informal survey among your Christian friends, asking them what they think God's forgiveness of sins in Christ means for politics and government.

If Christ has not been raised, your faith
is futile; you are still in your sins.

—1 Corinthians 15:17

- 28 -

MATURITY AND RIGHTEOUSNESS

Hebrews 5:12-6:3; 1 Thessalonians 5:21-23

For many Christians, faith is a matter of receiving forgiveness and then telling others about repentance from sin, turning to faith in God through Christ, being baptized, looking forward to the resurrection, and escaping eternal judgment. For many, these teachings exhaust the life of faith. Most of the Christians I meet think of worship, prayer, and evangelism as primary Christianity, while they view politics as irrelevant or relatively unimportant to the Christian life.

What a shock it is, then, to read the letter to the Hebrews where the writer calls these teachings "elementary." They are indeed essential teachings, just as milk is essential for an infant until it matures. But they are just the beginning teachings of the Christian faith. They are for the newborn and the immature. Their purpose is to bring one from the milk of spiritual immaturity to the solid food spiritual maturity.

Let us leave the elementary teachings about Christ and go on to maturity, not laying again the foundation of repentance from acts that lead to death, and of faith in God, instruction about baptisms, the laying on of hands, the resurrection of the dead, and eternal judgment.

—Hebrews 6:1-2

What then is solid food for a Christian? Hebrews says it is "the teaching about righteousness" (5:13)—the solid food for those "who by constant use have trained themselves to distinguish good from evil" (v. 14). In other words, Christians should move on to maturity in righteousness (6:1).

Paul says much the same thing to the Thessalonians. After trying to correct some misunderstandings about the meaning of the resurrection among those young Christians, Paul urges them to test everything, to hold on to the good, and to avoid every kind of evil (1 Thess. 5:21-22). Maturity means growth in discerning good from evil as part of one's growth in understanding righteousness.

Righteousness is God's right way for humans to live in the world. It is the right path of justice and peace and love that should govern every dimension of life, including the public dimensions. Righteousness is what God has now made possible for this world through his Son, Jesus Christ. Righteousness is the standard by which God judges all things. Those who are growing to maturity in Christ should be coming to an ever greater discernment of what is right and wrong for governments, for business enterprises, for schools, for families, for the media, as well as for their personal lives.

Righteousness in the affairs of this world is not a secondary or incidental matter for the Christian; it is the most important characteristic of maturity. We might restate the biblical command this way: "Don't forget to drink your milk, but don't hang onto the bottle all your life. Get on with it! Grow up! Learn to eat the meat of righteousness, which includes public justice."

REFLECTING . . .

- What is the biblical meaning of righteousness and justice? Why are they often used interchangeably in the Bible? How are they different?

- The next time a candidate running for public office mentions that he or she is a Christian, perhaps even a born-again Christian, ask yourself whether the testimony they give appears to be more of the "milk" or more of the "meat" variety.

ACTING . . .

- Reexamine your own spiritual diet. What do your daily faith practices, your work, your civic involvement say about your spiritual maturity?

May God himself, the God of peace, sanctify you through and through. May your whole spirit, soul and body be kept blameless at the coming of our Lord Jesus Christ.

—1 Thessalonians 5:23

- 29 -

THANKSGIVING FOR GOD'S JUSTICE

2 Thessalonians 1:1-12

Paul begins many of his letters by giving thanks to God for those to whom he is writing. His thanksgiving for the Thessalonian Christians is specifically tied to the display of God's justice.

We ought always to thank God for you . . .
because your faith is growing more and more, and
the love every one of you has for each other is
increasing. Therefore, among God's churches we
boast about your perseverance and faith in all the
persecutions and trials you are enduring. All this
is evidence that God's judgment is right.

—2 Thessalonians 1:3-5

At first hearing, this may sound strange. Why does Paul give thanks for God's justice? It would make sense, we might think, if Paul were to applaud the faith and love of the Thessalonians while condemning the injustice around them, even urging them to get organized so they could change the system that oppressed them.

But Paul is a realist, not an idealist. The Christians to whom he wrote had no freedom to organize a march on Rome and no money to pay a lobbyist to represent them in the imperial city. Paul's thanksgiving and encouragement are fueled by a long-term vision, not by a short-term calculation about the exercise of human power in one generation. Realism for Paul is grounded in the confidence that God's final judgment will set everything straight and balance creation's scales once and for all.

The Thessalonian Christians suffered unjustly, as Christ did, but in spite of that pain they grew in faith and love because of God's work in them. Consequently, an imbalance of undeserved persecution has built up in God's world, and it will have to be corrected when Christ returns. On the other side of the coin, those who are doing the persecuting are also creating an imbalance on the scales of justice by handing out undeserved penalties. God cannot accept such an imbalance.

Thus Paul concludes that the present imbalance is sufficient to prove that Christians will be counted worthy of God's kingdom and the ungodly persecutors will inherit God's wrath and condemnation. Why? Because in God's creation full justice must be established and all imbalances must be overcome.

We should not read these words as an admonition to sit passively on the sidelines waiting for Christ to return. If we can do something to correct injustice around us, we should do so. But all our work to promote justice in this world should be seen in the light of God's great plan and ultimate purposes in Christ. God alone can overcome every injustice; God alone can balance the scales of justice by stopping all persecution and rewarding those who have suffered unjustly.

Our efforts to promote justice function as a precious incense offered up to God in thanksgiving and as small showers of blessing on our neighbors. Yet they add up to only small dust on the scales of God's renewal of the creation. Even in pain and suffering we can give thanks to the God who is holding onto his faithful ones until the day when everything will be balanced and set straight.

REFLECTING . . .

- What do you think Paul means when he tells the Thessalonians that God will fulfill "every act prompted by your faith" (v. 11)?

- Think about the imbalances caused by injustice at your workplace, in your community, or in your nation. What encouragement does Paul's message give you—to endure, to try to change things, or to do a little of both?

ACTING . . .

- In response to the injustice you've identified, make a specific plan for the next week to endure, to begin to change things, or to do some of both. Ask at least one person to pray for you.

We constantly pray for you, that our God
may count you worthy of his calling.

—2 Thessalonians 1:11

- 30 -

REMEMBERING, CELEBRATING, ANTICIPATING

Nehemiah 8-10

Anniversary celebrations often display a definite biblical pattern. Those who celebrate the anniversary begin with praise and thanksgiving to God, who initiated an original event. Then they often relate the story of what transpired between that moment of origin and the present day. The pattern then moves to confession of sin and repentance, followed by thanksgiving for God's mercy and patience. Finally, the people conclude their celebration by rededicating themselves to serve the Lord until his kingdom is fulfilled.

In Nehemiah 8-10 we find a beautiful example of this pattern. The occasion is a celebration of God's creation and restoration of Israel. Nehemiah has come to Jerusalem to help Israel's returning exiles rebuild the wall. They are successful only because God has brought them back into the true way of life. Nehemiah reminds Israel that the Lord is the one who took them out of Egypt long before engineering the exodus from Babylon. Nehemiah and the people then celebrate the rebuilding of the wall, which represents the restoration of Israel after the exile. This in turn leads them to a rereading of the law.

---

*The whole company that had returned from exile. . . .
had not celebrated [the Feast of Tabernacles] like
this. And their joy was very great. Day after day,
from the first day to the last, Ezra read from the
Book of the Law of God.*

—Nehemiah 8:17-18

As Ezra and Nehemiah read the law of God and lead the people in a celebration of past and present events, they turn to God in worship, repeating the pattern outlined above: praise (8:6; 9:5-6), retelling the story (9:7-31), confession of sin (9:32-37), thanksgiving (9:32-33), and rededication (9:38; 10).

In 2002, the Center for Public Justice celebrates its 25th anniversary. The Center is, by all counts, a modest organization, not a state, not a church, not a major corporation. Nevertheless, as an association of Christian citizens dedicated to the service of God and neighbors by seeking justice in the public realm, we ought to follow this biblical pattern of celebration. In fact, in remembering our relatively short history, we should pause to reflect on the Preamble to our by-laws, which begins with praise to the Ruler and Judge of the earth, then moves to a confession of sin, and concludes with a dedication to serve God and neighbors with justice.

We have much for which to give thanks. God has encouraged us from the beginning to find new ways to work together for justice in the United States. Our accomplishments may be small and our failings great, but we celebrate this anniversary to remind ourselves once again that the Lord is the one who directs our paths, who forgives sins, and who will finally and completely establish justice and peace. The calling to which we rededicate ourselves is that of being faithful in seeking to do justice, in seeking to understand the implications of justice for all the details of public law and policy in the United States and the world today. God is patient. There is much work to be done until Christ returns.

REFLECTING . . .

- The return of the exiles to Jerusalem and the rebuilding of the wall did not come close to restoring Israel to its former glory. How could these events have anticipated God's final redemption of the faithful?

- Invite two or three people active in urban ministry to visit your adult education class or small group Bible study. Ask them what sins they see that Christians need to confess before God. What is it that they celebrate after years of service? What signs of hope and anticipation of God's final restoration do they see from their work?

ACTING . . .

- The next time your family celebrates a special occasion, set aside time to praise God, retell your family story, confess your sins, give thanks, and rededicate each person to God's service. Consider making this a meaningful ritual at every family celebration.

They stood in their places and confessed their
sins and the wickedness of their fathers.

—Nehemiah 9:2

JUSTICE ADMINISTERED

And what more shall I say? I do not have time to tell about Gideon, Barak, Samson, Jephthah, David, Samuel and the prophets, who through faith conquered kingdoms, administered justice, and gained what was promised; who shut the mouths of lions, quenched the fury of the flames, and escaped the edge of the sword; whose weakness was turned to strength; and who became powerful in battle and routed foreign armies. Women received back their dead, raised to life again. Others were tortured and refused to be released, so that they might gain a better resurrection. Some faced jeers and flogging, while still others were chained and put in prison.

—Hebrews 11:32-36

G od created human beings in the image of God and called them to administer justice on earth. Male and female in their generations would come to know both themselves and God in the course of following a just way of life, learning to govern rightly.

Doing justice is not something optional; it is not something to be chosen or neglected at will, without consequences. Humans will act either justly or unjustly. Either they will keep God's commandments and be blessed, or they will fail to keep the commandments and be cursed. Whether receiving blessings or suffering curses, humans cannot escape the responsibility God gave them. The demands of justice will stand.

The Mystery of Human Accountability

Yet how can humans administer justice if they themselves, through the disobedience of Adam and Eve, are cursed by God, alienated from divine fellowship, and implicated in the perpetration of injustice? How can the Creator be satisfied with the human administration of justice in creation when the administrators are mired in sin and bent on disobedience? What holds the creation together if there is no one other than God left to do justice?

God's way of dealing with fallen men and women is a mystery that has been unfolding through history and is now coming to full disclosure. Part of the story is God's persistence in being merciful to the creatures responsible for the administration of justice. The Lord has continued to treat men and women as creatures made in the image of God, not withdrawing responsibility and accountability from them. Yet, in the face of their disobedience, God has had to take decisive action to judge and redeem the world, including sinful humans, so that the creation can reach its sabbath fulfillment.

By upholding the creation with grace and mercy, the Lord has been at work exposing the difference between justice and injustice. Men and women, called to govern, have not been left in darkness without a witness to the truth about what God requires—God has given his Word.

The verses from the letter to the Hebrews remind us that many who lived by faith "administered justice." The author of Hebrews explains that Moses, the great administrator and judge of Israel, "was faithful as a servant in God's house, testifying to what would be said in the future" (3:5). David, Israel's greatest king, gave a picture of the Messiah to come. Many others were also faithful administrators in God's house. On the other hand, God condemned those kings of Israel who perpetuated injustice even while allowing them to remain on the throne for years at a time. The Lord's condemnation of unjust rulers contrasted sharply with his words of approval for those who pursued justice.

"Woe to him who builds his palace by unrighteousness, his upper rooms by injustice, making his countrymen work for nothing, not paying them for their labor. He says, 'I will build myself a great palace with spacious upper rooms.' So he makes large windows in it, panels it with cedar and decorates it in red. Does it make you a king to have more and more cedar? Did not your father [Josiah] have food and drink? He did what was right and just, so all went well with him. He defended the cause of the poor and needy, and so all went well. Is that not what it means to know me?" declares the LORD.

—Jeremiah 22:13-16

The record given us by Job, a great man of righteousness, looks back on his life from the standpoint of his later humiliation. Job recalled that his days of greatest joy and pleasure—his days of clearest self-knowledge and knowledge of God—were those when he sat in the city gate as an administrator of justice.

"Whoever heard me spoke well of me, and those who saw me commended me, because I rescued the poor

who cried for help, and the fatherless who had none
to assist him. . . . I put on righteousness as my
clothing; justice was my robe and my turban. . . .
I took up the case of the stranger. I broke the fangs of
the wicked and snatched the victims from their teeth."

—Job 29:11-17

The Responsibility of Administration

Many citizens of the United States hold a negative view of government and of public officials. Yet, if we take time to think about it, we can find many examples of judges, governors, public administrators, and citizens who, by God's grace, have taken up the cause of the stranger or helped break the fangs of the wicked in order to protect the innocent.

My friend Don Smarto, who worked for many years in the criminal justice system, endured great personal pain in order to contribute to the judicial administration of justice. Telling of his own traumatic experience when required to testify in the trial of his brother for bank robbery, he says:

> I will never forget walking out of that courtroom. There were no agents, not even the prosecutor to say thank you or good-by. I walked down a Chicago street, thinking about the Civil War and that I understood now how brothers could end up on different sides of a conflict. But I knew I was not angry at God, even though I was questioning the whole affair. I didn't understand how he would use this, but I understood clearly who was responsible. I hung on to the simple belief that followers of Christ were not to lie. Although I had witnessed a lot of untruthfulness on the witness stand over the years, I had no choice but to take that oath seriously.

—Don Smarto, *Pursued*
(InterVarsity Press, 1990) p. 190.

By pointing to the requirements of justice while calling human beings to their inescapable responsibility, God has been revealing the truth about both the Creator and the creation, about both God and the image of God. Justice has to do with the way human beings live in relation to God, to one another, and to the rest of the creation. It has to do, for example, with how we deal with the poor and the needy, the stranger and the oppressed, the thief and the murderer.

The Scriptures also make clear that the inescapable responsibility of administering justice belongs not only to God's chosen people, not only to those who thankfully receive the Lord's redeeming grace. *Every* man and woman throughout the human generations stands accountable before God. Thus, when Jesus stood before Pilate, even Pilate's power was granted by God. Even though Pilate had no faith in God, he could not escape his accountability to God for the administration of justice.

"Do you refuse to speak to me?" Pilate said.
"Don't you realize I have power either to
free you or to crucify you?"

Jesus answered, "You would have no power over
me if it were not given to you from above."

—John 19:10-11

The apostle Paul reminded the Roman Christians to submit to human government because it is established by God. This is not to say that everything each ruler does is just and proper. Rather, it is to say that the authority to administer justice is God-given. Regardless of whether a ruler is elected or not, a follower of Jesus Christ or an atheist, that person bears responsibility from God to administer justice.

"Everyone must submit himself to the governing
authorities, for there is no authority except that
which God has established. The authorities that
exist have been established by God."

—Romans 13:1

Our Representative

For his part, Jesus submitted to "jeers and flogging" (Heb. 11:36) in order to fulfill his Father's just condemnation of disobedient men and women. Jesus testified to the requirements of God's justice even as he collapsed under the weight of Pilate's unfair trial. For the love of both God and the human creatures with whom he cast his lot, Jesus accepted the penalty of God's verdict against sin.

However, the prophetic words Jesus spoke to Pilate about his own kingship were fulfilled when the Father accepted Jesus as the representative human administrator of justice for the whole creation and unleashed the Holy Spirit on the earth at Pentecost. The complete manifestation of Jesus' kingship has not yet come, but when it does, the truth that his administration encompasses the entire creation will be made known.

Jesus said, "My kingdom is not of this world
. . . my kingdom is from another place."

"You are a king, then!" said Pilate.

Jesus answered, "You are right in saying that I am a
king. In fact, for this reason I was born, and for this
I came into the world, to testify to the truth.
Everyone on the side of truth listens to me."

—John 18:36-37

As the Lord walks with men and women through history, the drama of human justice and injustice reveals with increasing clarity who God is and who we are. And one day we will experience the final outcome of the drama when God's chosen and approved Judge, Jesus Christ, opens all the books and settles all accounts (Rev. 11:15-18). In him and through him our earthly responsibility for the administration of justice will be fulfilled.

REFLECTING . . .

* Read the biblical story of Deborah, Gideon, Barak, Samson, or Jephthah in the book of Judges and note the ways in which she or he administered justice.

* Why do you think God's praise of just actions and condemnation of unjust actions play such a prominent role in the story of God's saving work in history?

* The political systems of most Western countries divide, to some degree, the powers of legislation, adjudication, and executive administration. In what respects do you believe this aids or hinders the administration of justice?

ACTING . . .

- Write a note of appreciation or make a phone call to thank a public official for standing up for justice. Keep that person in your prayers.

JUSTICE HAPPENING

Lyman Howell, regional consultant for the Christian Reformed World Relief Committee (CRWRC), is comfortable talking about money. With an MBA in finance, the ins and outs of banking don't get him down. Lyman also knows the poor in society, and he's attempting to provide them access to powerful social institutions like banks.

Lyman is guided by Jesus' announcement that he came to bring "good news to the poor" (Luke 4:18), a quote from Isaiah 61. In that passage, Isaiah says that the oppressed "will be called oaks of righteousness . . . they will rejoice in their inheritance . . . 'for I, the LORD, love justice'" (Isa. 61:3, 7-8).

But how will justice happen? How can the poor and oppressed share in the wealth of our country? These are the questions Lyman seeks to answer. He says:

> While working with community groups in Chicago on issues related to bank mergers, I was exposed to the tremendous resources and loan money available. We have massive growth in wealth in this country—but only for certain people. Others are living hand to mouth, isolated from the system. I wanted to bring this issue to the banking community. I wanted to say, "Let's work things out together."
>
> A lot of savings programs are for the middle and upper class. Why can't we have savings programs that serve the poor? Many of the poor are without bank accounts and have no relationship with a bank. People with no financial literacy easily fall victim to predatory lenders—the corner check cashers, the quick-loan folks.

That's why Lyman is working with a coalition of Christian ministries in Indiana. They have been able to claim 32 percent of the state's allocation of matching grant monies to fund Individual Development Accounts for the poor. IDAs encourage low income families to save for education, transportation, housing, or starting a small business; their savings are matched with money from the state's allocation of monies to community organizations who work with these families.

Lyman has found a way to work with others to enable struggling families to share in the wealth of our country. "All who see them will acknowledge that they [both giver and receiver] are a people the LORD has blessed" (Isa. 61:9).

MEDITATIONS 31-45

- 31 -

RENDER TO CAESAR

Matthew 22:15-22

One of the most frequently quoted passages of Scripture on politics is Jesus' response to a question about paying taxes. To understand Jesus' mandate, we must recognize that the context is dramatic. Jesus is not giving a lecture on political theory. His statement is very compact and without elaboration, simply a response to the Pharisees and Herodians, who are trying to trap him into saying something that will violate either his obligation to God or his duty toward Caesar. Jesus sees through his questioners and speaks to their evil intent: "You hypocrites, why are you trying to trap me?" (Matt. 22:18).

"Give to Caesar what is Caesar's,
and to God what is God's."

—Matthew 22:21

The brief episode concludes with Jesus confounding his opponents by tangling them in their false dilemma. Matthew says, "When they heard this, they were amazed. So they left him and went away" (v. 22). No questions, no argument. Anything they might have said would have created more problems for them than for Jesus.

What is so profound about Jesus' statement that it silenced even his enemies? Jesus sets the tone with his initial words, addressing the inquisitors as "hypocrites." The simple phrase that follows is loaded with meaning: "Give to Caesar what rightfully belongs to him, including the coin with his image on it. Use it to pay the taxes due him. It's not everything, but it's important. But then open your eyes! Don't you see what properly belongs to God? You owe everything to God, including all that you give to Caesar. Give God yourselves—the *coin* that has God's image on it——the whole of your life."

The Pharisees and Herodians were hung! Jesus had not challenged the authority of Caesar; the Herodians could not get him for that. And the Pharisees certainly were not ready to let Jesus lead a discussion about serving God with all one's heart, soul, and strength. So they all went away.

In the light of other Scripture passages we can, of course, read more into this statement. Giving Caesar what belongs to him is much the same as giving parents or teachers or any other human authority what belongs to them—the "authorities" are always under God. In the context of God's kingdom, even the most powerful Caesar has relatively little authority. The real weight of Jesus' command is that God's authority holds every official and every person in every office accountable to God. Even Caesar exists and rules by the grace of God.

If we serve God in all things, then we'll know when to obey and when not to obey Caesar. Our "taxes" for Caesar must serve God's will. God gives Caesar his limited authority because God continues to hold humans accountable to administer justice in creation. Caesar, on the other hand, does not define the limits of God's authority.

Amazing, isn't it, how much Jesus could put into a dozen words!

_____

REFLECTING . . .

- Why do you think this famous passage is so often interpreted as if Caesar gets what is secular and God gets what is sacred?

- What is good and bad about the phrase "In God we trust" on some American coins?

ACTING . . .

- As you note the deductions from your next paycheck, pray that God will use your taxes to administer justice in creation.

_____

"Teacher, we know you are a man of integrity
and that you teach the way of God in
accordance with the truth."

—Matthew 22:16

_____

- 32 -
SHARED ADMINISTRATION OF JUSTICE
Exodus 18:1-27

God's liberation of Israel from Egypt could hardly have been a more authoritarian act. God simply overruled an oppressive Pharaoh, who mistakenly believed that he had unlimited authority, and set Israel free.

In contrast, it's worth noticing how God guided Israel into a form of society characterized by widely shared responsibility for the administration of justice. God did not set Moses up as a new pharaoh. Rather, he used Moses to show Israel how to administer justice, which never permits human authorities to act as if they are God.

Long before Israel entered the promised land, when God was still purging them of bad habits and directing their desert march, God showed Moses that justice could not be done if all the reins of power remained in his hands. Imagine the burden for justice Moses would have carried if God had not taught him this lesson early.

At this early point in the Israelites' journey, Moses' father-in-law, Jethro, a priest of Midian, visits Moses. Jethro is impressed by every-thing God is doing for Israel. He watches Moses at work settling disputes among the people and pointing them to God's path for life. But Jethro soon becomes concerned. Moses is trying to do all the judging single-handedly. It's not good for Moses or the people.

So Jethro jumps in to ask, "What is this you are doing for the people? Why do you alone sit as judge, while all these people stand around you from morning till evening?" (Ex. 18:14).

Moses explains that he has to exercise such authority because "the people come to me to seek God's will. Whenever they have a dispute, it is brought to me, and I decide between the parties and inform them of God's decrees and laws" (vv. 15-16).

Jethro spots the error in Moses' reasoning. God did, of course, use Moses authoritatively to lead Israel out of Egypt. Moses, as chief judge, has to administer justice. But Jethro sees that Moses cannot handle this alone. He gives Moses a piece of sound fatherly advice: "Lighten the load!"

"Select capable men . . . who fear God, trustworthy
men . . . and appoint them as officials over
thousands, hundreds, fifties, tens. Have them serve

*as judges for the people at all times, but have them
bring every difficult case to you; the simple cases
they can decide themselves."*

—Exodus 18:21-22

No human authority can administer all the demands of justice for a complex society. A just political order requires the service of many capable and qualified people who fear God, who are trustworthy, and who hate dishonest gain. Today we take for granted representative government and various constitutional and judicial safeguards. But it seems that we've largely forgotten that the widespread dispersal of human authority is a gift from God—from the only one who may rightfully claim to be tireless in the administration of justice and limitless in authority.

REFLECTING . . .

- Why do you think God used Jethro, a non-Israelite, to speak this truth to Moses?

- Ask a state or federal judge to explain how the court system is organized to allow for the distribution of cases from simplest to most difficult and for the review of one judge's (or jury's) decision by another?

ACTING . . .

- Covenant with your spouse, fellow employees, neighbors, or members of your church to share the load for a specific work of justice you are trying to accomplish.

*"That will make your load lighter,
because they will share it with you."*

—Exodus 18:22

- 33 -

TAX TIME

Romans 13:5-7

In Romans 13, Paul explains that we pay taxes because "the authorities are God's servants, who give their full time to governing" (Rom. 13:6). In other words, those whom God has appointed to govern deserve to be supported with the taxes that make their service possible.

Taxation is not theft. Government has a rightful claim to taxes. We owe government these monies because government is God's servant called to administer justice. Our response, then, should not be a grudging payment merely so we can avoid arrest, but rather, a thankful payment of what is owed.

Give everyone what you owe him: If you owe taxes,
pay taxes; if revenue, then revenue; if respect,
then respect; if honor, then honor.

—Romans 13:7

But how do we determine what is "owed"? What constitutes a just system of taxation? How should God's full-time government servants govern justly? When Paul describes our duty, he doesn't address in any detail our questions. Clearly, Paul is not writing an essay on political obligation and public administration. Paul did not say many things that he could have said. These few verses in Romans come in the context of Paul's deep desire to show Christians how to live in this world—by the law of love rather than by the law of vengeance. The obligation to honor God's servants is simply part of that larger responsibility to live as people who owe others nothing but love.

We need not speculate about what Paul thought government should do or about how he might have evaluated the Roman tax system in his day. Paul was a Jew who knew the Torah and the Prophets inside and out. Judges and law courts had an important place in God's ordering of Israel's life. Paul was well trained in the execution of government.

Like Paul, we have a responsibility to understand our tax system and the way our government functions. We must take time to discuss these matters with fellow believers and ask questions: Are our tax dollars being collected fairly? Do we need a new and better tax code? Are the governing authorities using these taxes to govern justly? If you conclude that improvement is needed, don't get angry about paying taxes or demand that taxes be reduced. Instead, get busy as citizens—as public servants of the Lord—to convince those who govern to spend their time doing justice instead of injustice.

REFLECTING . . .

- What is the philosophy behind the slogan "taxation is theft"? Why is it incompatible with biblical teaching?

- Meditate on the task God has given the authorities to whom you send your taxes. (To understand Paul's Old Testament perspective, read Deuteronomy 1:9-18 about God's appointment of governing authorities for Israel, 14:22-29 about the meaning of the tithe, and 16:18-20 and 17:8-13 about the role of judges and the courts of law in Israel.)

ACTING . . .

- Read a book or attend a class about different kinds of taxes (property tax, income tax, sales tax, users tax, value-added tax, and so on). What are the merits and limits or disadvantages of each kind? What are the criteria by which a means of taxation should be judged? Are there injustices you feel called to change?

Therefore, it is necessary to submit to the
authorities, not only because of possible
punishment but also because of conscience.

—Romans 13:5

34

MIGHTY KING OR MAD COW?

Daniel 4:24-27

Daniel's life was defined by politics—the politics of Israel's long captivity in Babylon. At a relatively young age he rose to a position equivalent to the prime minister of Babylon. The apocalyptic visions, the miraculous events, and the interpretations of dreams recorded in his book all revolve around the power struggles and political intrigues of that amazing, ancient superpower.

Daniel and his young Hebrew friends demonstrated their courage and faith right from the start of their exile in Babylon.

One night early in their captivity, King Nebuchadnezzar, having recognized the connection between Daniel's keen insights and Israel's God, calls upon Daniel to interpret a dream. Daniel's response brings into sharp focus two elements of "power politics" that are fundamental and always connected in biblical revelation—elements that are as important for the Babylonians as they were for Israel.

First, Daniel asserts that the relation between even the highest human political authority and God is a relation of human subordination to the Most High. God is supreme; the human office holder always stands at God's disposal and exercises authority only by delegation from God. "O King," says Daniel, "you [must] acknowledge that the Most High is sovereign over the kingdoms of men and gives them to anyone he wishes" (Dan. 4:25).

Second, Daniel explains what God requires of a king. Merely expressing a few pious words at a royal prayer breakfast and tipping one's crown to God are never sufficient to please the Lord of heaven and earth. Daniel advises, "Renounce your sins by doing what is right, and your wickedness by being kind to the oppressed" (v. 27).

The king's dream comes true, as Daniel has foretold. Nebuchadnezzar goes mad and ends up living like a wild animal, eating grass, his hair growing "like the feathers of an eagle and his nails like the claws of a bird" (v. 33). Then, one day, by God's grace, the king wakes up from his insanity, raises his eyes to heaven, and praises the God of Daniel. His kingdom is restored to him, and he declares his loyalty to the sovereign God.

Daniel had learned that God's chosen people do not have to remain a separate, self-ruled nation in order for God to be God. Certainly Nebuchadnezzar or any other ruler should learn the same. God is not impressed by earthly glory.

Rather, the Most High, the Sovereign over all rulers, is impressed with the administration of justice, mercy, and kindness to the oppressed. Thus, for the lowest magistrate or the highest king, Daniel's words convey these marching orders from God: Recognize that the Lord is King above all kings. Do justice. Look after the oppressed. Everything else will lead to destruction.

"Now I, Nebuchadnezzar, praise and exalt and glorify the King of heaven, because everything he does is right and all his ways are just. And those who walk in pride he is able to humble."

—Daniel 4:37

REFLECTING . . .

- Think about King Nebuchadnezzar's conversion experience. What characterized it? Why would God allow a Babylonian king to become a believer?

- Recall one incident in the history of your country that demonstrated a political turn from pride to humility before God, whether on the part of a political leader, the laws, or the constitution. Why did it happen?

ACTING . . .

- Spend time praying that you and those in authority over you may be humble before God.

He does as he pleases with the powers of heaven and the peoples of the earth.

—Daniel 4:35

- 35 -

NATURAL LAW

Romans 1:18-2:16; Acts 26:1-29

The apostle Paul, like the Old Testament prophets, had no doubt that God's order for creation holds all human beings accountable. The standards or principles by which human actions must be judged are universally evident even for those who do not know God's law.

Indeed, when Gentiles, who do not have the law, do by nature things required by the law, they are a law for themselves, even though they do not have the law, since they show that the requirements of the law are written on their hearts.

—Romans 2:14-15

However, unlike many of the Greek and Roman philosophers of his day, Paul did not hold out hope that human beings in general, by reason alone, would grasp and obey natural law. The fact that God's law holds for everyone does not mean that everyone believes, accepts, understands, and agrees to obey it.

To the contrary, even though everyone is "without excuse" because "what may be known about God is plain" to see, sinful people neither glorify God nor give God thanks, and their thinking becomes futile and their hearts darkened (Rom. 1:18-21). "They have become filled with every kind of wickedness, evil, greed and depravity," Paul writes. "They are full of envy, murder, strife, deceit and malice. They are gossips, slanderers, God-haters, insolent, arrogant and boastful; they invent ways of doing evil; they disobey their parents; they are senseless, faithless, heartless, ruthless" (vv. 29-31).

What is Paul's answer to this predicament? Does he give up on the universal embrace of God's law-ordered creation and on human rationality? Not at all. But neither does he believe that human beings, in the darkness of sin, can reach a common, rational agreement about what the law says and demands. The problem is not with God's creation order but with disobedient hearts and minds that no longer hold the truth or abide by the law.

That, says Paul, during his trial before King Agrippa, is why God sent Jesus Christ into the world. The law is not at fault, but sinful people will not obey it. The light of Christ sustains God's good law-order for creation and exposes darkened hearts so repentant sinners can once again see the truth and goodness of that law.

As we work for the truth and goodness of the law today, whether in legislatures or before courts and kings, let us pray for opportunities to respond as Paul did to King Agrippa's question, "Do you think that in such a short time you can persuade me to be a Christian?" Paul replied, "I pray God that not only you but all who are listening to me today may become what I am, except for these chains" (Acts 26:28-29).

REFLECTING . . .

- What would be a good example today of a moral law of creation that most people acknowledge but which some reject or resist because of darkened hearts?

- Many political disputes occur today over public or political morality. What is the difference between those issues that are disputed because people disagree about what is moral and those clearly immoral issues over which there is disagreement about whether government is responsible to enforce the moral law?

ACTING . . .

- Look around your community today for evidences that God's law is practiced even by those who do not know God in Jesus Christ. Rejoice when civic and religious organizations unite to care for the poor and show other acts of love, and volunteer to work for such causes.

"I am saying nothing beyond what the prophets and
Moses said would happen—that the Christ would
suffer and, as the first to rise from the dead,
would proclaim light to his own people
and to the Gentiles."

—Acts 26:22-23

- 36 -

WISDOM AND POLITICS

Proverbs 11:14; 15:22; 27:17

It would seem that President Reagan wisely followed the words of Proverbs about seeking counsel as the secret Iranian arms deal began to unravel late in 1986. Yet Reagan's policy of secretly shipping arms to Iran was a serious mistake, and using those sales as the source of funds for Nicaraguan Contras was utterly foolish. Plans fail, and a nation can fall as a result.

For lack of guidance a nation falls,
but many advisers make victory sure.

Plans fail for lack of counsel,
but with many advisers they succeed.

—Proverbs 11:14; 15:22

The reason for the Reagan administration's errors appeared to be that the President had too many advisers rather than too few. Hundreds of people worked closely with the President in the White House, and since he freely delegated responsibility, it wasn't possible to keep track of all those advisers. Conventional wisdom would seem to suggest that if the President had been surrounded by only a few advisers rather than by hundreds, he might not have fallen into that destructive and scandalous affair.

But take another look at the two proverbs. They are not mistaken and old-fashioned. They illuminate the Washington landscape as sharply today as they did Jerusalem's in King Solomon's time.

What actually did happen at the White House? A very small number of deputies, shielded by the president's office and acting outside the limits of their authority, tried to carry out plans that were not approved, or even considered, by some of the most important officials in the State Department, the Pentagon, and Congress. The President's error was not in having too many advisers. Rather, it was in allowing a few of the wrong people to act without advice from the many who were appointed and elected for precisely that purpose.

The American political system is one in which many officials and advisers are legally required to take part in policy making. One of the reasons we have such a system is the long-standing objection to arbitrary government by monarchs and unrepresentative parliaments—a reaction that began with the founding of the American colonies. Our system is designed to make conformity with the wisdom of these proverbs possible. *Many* advisers are necessary for success.

REFLECTING . . .

- Do you think that elected representatives to contemporary legislatures and parliaments can be considered "advisers" as that word is used in these two proverbs?

- When is it appropriate to seek out private advice in contrast to public advice at a hearing or in a committee meeting? Why?

ACTING . . .

- Ask your family members or close friends how they think these proverbs might apply to circumstances at home, in the church, among friends, on the job, or at school. Agree to seek each other's counsel before making important decisions.

As iron sharpens iron, so one man sharpens another.

—Proverbs 27:17

- 37 -

PATIENCE OR PRESSURE FOR UNJUST RULERS?

1 Samuel 24:1-22

In the 1990s, many, if not most, Americans were convinced that Saddam Hussein, who ruled Iraq, and Slobodan Milosevic, who ruled what was left of Yugoslavia, should be forced from power. Before that, it was Panama's General Manuel Noriega. For decades, Cuba's Fidel Castro has been considered an illegitimate ruler.

Are these convictions justified? What is the proper starting point for a strategy that seeks to force an end to tyranny or to highly unjust governments?

Young David's response to King Saul should get our attention. By the time Saul fell into David's hands in a cave near the desert of En Gedi, God had already revealed that David would be Israel's next king and that God no longer favored Saul. Moreover, Saul had been trying to kill David—not just once, but repeatedly. Surely the Lord would side with David if he killed Saul, thereby putting an end to his increasingly miserable and arbitrary regime. But, no, David refused to take Saul's life when it seemed so obviously right to do so.

Notice carefully the force of David's actions as well as his motivation. David understood that the real struggle was not between himself and Saul. God is the one who sets up and throws down kings. David knew that his own kingship was a gift from God, not something of his own making. God could dispose of David for his pride and impatience as easily as he could dispose of Saul. The key to action, then, has to be humility before God.

However, David's humility consisted of more than passive waiting. He put great pressure on Saul by cutting off a piece of the king's robe and with his strong words.

"May the LORD judge between you and me. And may the Lord avenge the wrongs you have done to me, but my hand will not touch you. . . . Against whom has the king of Israel come out? Whom are you pursuing? A dead dog? A flea? May the LORD be our judge and decide between us. May he consider

my cause and uphold it, may he vindicate me
by delivering me from your hand."

—1 Samuel 24:12, 14-15

David did not ease up on Saul, but neither did he act as if he were Saul's highest judge. Ultimately, Saul had to confront God, not David. God would avenge David, if David were right. While it's true that nothing can justify tyrannical rulers and evil regimes, it is also true that the standard of judgment has to be God's and not merely our own.

As God gives us light to understand justice, we should never tolerate the injustice we see and wait passively for someone else to do something about it. We should confront rather than cooperate with unjust rulers, refusing to accept injustice as God's will simply because a government is doing it. Military response to a murderous regime is not necessarily wrong. But the kind of pressure we put on unjust rulers and regimes should be the kind that calls both us and them to account before the King of kings.

REFLECTING . . .

- What differences are there between David's relation to Saul and NATO's relation to Serbia's Milosevic?

- Think about elections and other contemporary means used to select people who hold offices of authority in government, the church, business, and nonprofit organizations. How do we acknowledge God's authorization and appointment using these methods?

ACTING . . .

- Think of a situation where you have simply put up with injustice, waiting passively for someone else to act. What are you willing to do to confront those involved? Plan how and when you will take the first step.

"I will not lift up my hand against my master,
because he is the LORD's anointed."

—1 Samuel 24:10

- 38 -

THE SONG OF DEBORAH

Judges 5:1-31

The stories about Israel during the time of the judges, right after they entered Canaan, are filled with grand acts of vengeance and tribal warfare. The Song of Deborah offers praise to God following one such act—when Jael, the wife of Heber, managed to kill Sisera, the commander of a Canaanite army that had cruelly oppressed Israel for twenty years.

After Jael had lured Sisera into her tent, "her hand reached for the tent peg, her right hand for the workman's hammer. She struck Sisera, she crushed his head, she shattered and pierced his temple. At her feet he sank, he fell; there he lay. At her feet he sank, he fell; where he sank, there he fell—dead."

[Deborah sang:] "So may all your enemies perish, O LORD! But may they who love you be like the sun when it rises in its strength."

—Judges 5:26-27, 31

Today we tend to react to these stories in one of two ways: either with horror or with a secret wish that we could do the same to our enemies. Both reactions miss the point of the story and the meaning of the times. To be sure, Jael's murder of Sisera was horrible, as was Sisera's oppression of Israel. We should be thankful that God has now made clear in Jesus Christ that vengeance belongs to him and not to us.

But at the same time, we should not think that retribution is no longer relevant to God's purposes. We may still pray that God's enemies will perish if they do not repent so that those who love God may shine like the sun in peace and strength. Yet we are mistaken if, in our prayer for justice, we assume that our country or our group of believers is God's instrument for vengeance and that everyone else is God's enemy.

Neither the Christian faithful nor a particular state or nation is God's chosen means of vengeance against his enemies. We too are

subject to God's judgment. No one on earth has sufficient righteousness to justify throwing the first stone.

In God's timing, Sisera's judgment was deserved, and Jael was
God's instrument. But also in God's timing, Jesus Christ has been
revealed as the supreme judge, the Messiah of God who will return in
final judgment. Thus, no person or nation or organization today may
legitimately claim to be God's vengeance squad. God has identified
the authoritative judge, and for the sake of Jesus Christ we have been
called to leave vengeance in God's hands.

REFLECTING . . .

- How can one justify both Jael's treatment of Sisera and David's
  treatment of King Saul (see meditation 37)? Could God have
  approved both?

- Explore with friends or in a small group the contemporary debates
  over capital punishment. What are its biblical grounds? Why
  might one contend today that capital punishment by legitimate
  state authority should continue, or, on the other hand, that it
  should no longer be used?

ACTING . . .

- Confess any secret wish you harbor that those with whom you
  disagree or those who have treated you unfairly would be avenged.

"I will make music to the LORD, the God of Israel."

—Judges 5:3

- 39 -

GOOD STEWARDSHIP
AND DANGEROUS LUXURY

Matthew 25:14-30; James 5:1-6

Anyone who has heard the parable of the talents knows that a good steward is one who produces wealth with his original capital. And anyone who has read James knows that the production of wealth will not save anyone. Riches are not the chief end of life; in fact, wealth can easily lead one to mistreat others and therefore suffer God's judgment.

"Look! The wages you failed to pay the
workmen who mowed your fields are crying out
against you. The cries of the harvesters have reached
the ears of the Lord Almighty. You have lived
on earth in luxury and self-indulgence."

—James 5:4

What are the implications of these teachings, if any, for government's economic policies today? Should government's goal be to keep everyone equally poor in order to keep people away from the danger of luxury? Or should it encourage maximum production and consumption? Is it good for society to produce wealth as long as Christians avoid it? Or should Christians lead the way in wealth production in order to demonstrate good stewardship?

During the last few decades in the United States, the rich have been getting richer and the poor poorer. What should we do? What constitutes a just economy? Some Christians argue that individuals should share their resources voluntarily and that government should not use redistributive tax policies to "steal" from the rich in order to give to the poor. Other Christians believe that the quest for maximum profit is bad morality, but since it makes the economy function most efficiently, then Christians should function by one standard in their personal lives and by another standard in public life. Still other Christians are convinced that government should operate with a primary concern for overcoming poverty and economic inequality even if this requires a heavy hand from government to redistribute wealth.

A debate over these opinions is absolutely essential today. We should rethink our tax policies, welfare programs, and business activities that have succeeded and failed in the past. Moreover, we should give serious attention to the effect of government's policies on charity, productivity, and employment. We urgently need this debate, especially among Christians, because Christians profess that God calls public authorities to administer justice.

While we conduct this debate and search for better answers and policies, we should thoroughly examine biblical teaching, from the old covenant's law to the epistle of James, from the prophets to the gospel of Jesus Christ. The Bible is loaded with wisdom and instruction about the meaning of wealth and stewardship in God's sight and about the meaning of a public order that does justice to the economic responsibility of both individuals and institutions.

And when the debate is over, when we have finished making our policy proposals, our answers should stand up to the admonitions of both Matthew and James.

REFLECTING . . .

• How do you think these two passages fit together?

• Invite to your small group or church education class public office-holders and representatives of Christian civic organizations that take different approaches to economic justice. Ask them how they relate these two passages of Scripture and how they justify their economic policy proposals.

ACTING . . .

• Reexamine your own stewardship practices in light of these passages from Matthew and James.

"For everyone who has will be given more, and he will have an abundance."

—Matthew 25:29

- 40 -
GOD'S POWER OVER OUR KINGDOMS

Daniel 6:1-18

Much of our civic responsibility is, and should be, directed toward the change of unjust laws. Yet frequently we experience a terrible sense of frustration over the impenetrable or incorrigible political system. We feel powerless against the weight of traditions, bureaucracies, and powerful interest groups. Change does not come easily.

Daniel 6 tells a wonderful story about the meaning of human power and powerlessness.

By God's grace and rich blessing, Daniel has risen to the height of power in Babylon where he and other Jews live in exile. He has become one of the chief administrators of the whole country under King Darius. The king himself is so powerful, it seems he can do anything he wants. Yet Darius and Daniel become entangled in a ghastly predicament due to the prideful tradition of a kingdom that thinks itself immutable and eternal.

The tradition works this way: if the king makes a decree, it is fixed without any possibility of change, as if God had decreed it. In other words, the "constitution" cannot be amended. No court may rule on the matter. An all-powerful king can put his foot in his mouth and never get it out again. That is just what happens to Darius.

While Darius has the highest regard for Daniel, several other officials are jealous of the young Jew. So they trick the king into making a decree that will force Daniel's death. They ask the king to declare that no one may pray to any god other than the king himself. The king, flattered by this attentiveness to his godly power, signs the decree.

"Anyone who prays to any god or man during the next thirty days, except to you, O king; shall be thrown into the lions' den. Now, O king, issue the decree and put it in writing so that it cannot be altered."

—Daniel 5:7-8

The officials then go to Daniel's house to watch him pray—as he always does—to the God of Abraham, Isaac, and Jacob. Quickly they report Daniel's "ungodliness" to the king. Darius suddenly realizes that he has made a mistake. But it's too late. The king must bow before his own foolish decree because it was published "in accordance with the laws of the Medes and Persians, which cannot be repealed" (v. 8).

Darius is reduced to powerlessness. Daniel is thrown into the lions' den. But Daniel knows something that Darius does not know. The God of Abraham, Isaac, and Jacob, the God of the covenants, is not bound by the laws of the Medes and Persians. God raises up and throws down any kingdom he pleases. The audacious, pretentious tradition of the Medes and Persians is a lie, a myth, a testimony to false gods. Darius and his cunning officials have a big lesson to learn.

REFLECTING . . .

- In the past two decades, more and more members of the U.S. Congress have decided not to seek election to another term because of frustration and a sense of powerlessness. Why do you think they have felt this way?

- What traditions in the church community can prevent leaders from acting justly?

ACTING . . .

- Make a phone call or send an e-mail or letter to a government official who has recently taken a stand for justice. Offer your encouragement and prayers.

"May your God, whom you serve
continually, rescue you!"

—Daniel 6:16

- 41 -

HUNGRY LIONS AND THE ADMINISTRATION OF JUSTICE

Daniel 6:19-28

Babylon's King Darius, who appears to be all-powerful, suddenly finds himself powerless to do anything to save his friend Daniel. He can find no escape from the trap his counselors set for him. Once believing himself to be as immutable and powerful as the laws of the Medes and Persians, Darius soon discovers that he is actually a helpless slave to those laws. He cannot even change his own decrees. He has taken his tradition too seriously. Now he can do nothing. Daniel will be devoured.

But Daniel, who appears to be utterly powerless before King Darius and the laws of the Medes and Persians, prays to the Lord above Darius, to the King of kings, who rules and overrules all human decrees. And God answers.

What a revelation to King Darius when he arrives at the lions' den the next morning to discover that Daniel is alive! Only then does Darius see the truth. Not only is his power limited; even the "laws of the Medes and Persians" are limited. God has just annulled one of them. God can devour human laws just as the lions devour the devious officials whom the king throws into the lions' den.

One of the great and wonderful surprises of this story is that Darius, having seen the truth, accepts his humiliation with joy. He gains a liberating insight: he is not supreme. He welcomes the truth that the God of Israel, Daniel's God, is Lord over the whole earth. Quickly, Darius issues a new decree, a thanksgiving proclamation fit for mere humans: "to all the peoples . . . of every language throughout the land . . . I issue a decree that . . . people must fear and reverence the God of Daniel" (Dan. 6:25-26).

"For he [the God of Daniel] is the living God and
he endures forever; his kingdom will not be
destroyed, his dominion will never end. He
rescues and he saves; he performs signs and
wonders in the heavens and on the earth. He has
rescued Daniel from the power of the lions."

—Daniel 6:26-27

Daniel's faith was not kept private while he went about a "secular" career in politics. Daniel served one God both privately and publicly. His service to Darius all along was a service to God. By a miracle, Darius woke up to this truth, finally realizing that he could fill his office properly only by honoring God in all things, as Daniel did.

REFLECTING . . .

- Why does the knowledge of one's limits bring liberation and joy?

- What politician today do you think best reflects service to God in both private and public life?

ACTING . . .

- Encourage teachers in your church or in the Christian school in your community to add the political dimension to this story along with the usual focus on the miracle of the tamed lions and Daniel's faith. Better yet, volunteer to tell this story in the first person, taking the role of either Daniel or Darius—or tell it to your children or grandchildren.

"[The lions] have not hurt me, because
I was found innocent in [God's] sight."

—Daniel 6:22

- 42 -

SPEAK UP FOR ALL WHO ARE DESTITUTE

Proverbs 31:8-9; Matthew 25:40

Most of us have received motherly advice at some time in our lives. In Proverbs 31, a king whose name is Lemuel is advised by his mother to do what is right, to administer justice. Above all, this means doing right by the poor and the needy.

Speak up for those who cannot speak for themselves,
for the rights of all who are destitute. Speak up and
judge fairly; defend the rights of the poor and needy.

—Proverbs 31:8-9

Should we, in our day, take this advice as a command to maintain public welfare programs? The strongest argument I know against government aid to the poor is that it does injustice to both the recipient and the rest of society. The welfare recipient, according to this argument, becomes dependent on the handout, while working citizens end up paying for that unproductive dependency.

There is some truth to this argument, at least to the extent that it points to the danger of bad welfare programs. The argument is parallel to one which parents must consider in raising children: don't spoil your children by providing care and services that they can provide for themselves. A twenty-year-old who cannot brush his teeth or make his bed or get a job is not a healthy person. Not all "care" is good care.

At the same time, we know that any person's maturation becomes possible only because many people help raise, nurture, and support that person. Moms and dads raise children; teachers facilitate learning; city workers plow the streets, put out fires, and keep the sewers running. Even in our maturity, we all remain dependent on employers, judges, tax collectors, legislators, police, friends, and neighbors.

The point is that mature independence is never total self-sufficiency. No one really earns his or her own way entirely. Have you thought recently about the fact that bankruptcy laws allow a business to escape its debts if it is deeply enough in trouble? And what about the tax write-offs for those who have enough income to be able to use them, or the price supports for certain kinds of agricultural commodities, or the roads that are built for anyone with a car to use? No business or individual could stay alive in the United States today if government did not provide support. Even the criminal in prison is given food and clothing.

Yes, we can do without bad welfare programs that create degrading dependencies. But we cannot have public justice without government protection of the neediest citizens. If government can direct its efforts so that the necessary care can be provided entirely by families, churches, private charities, and businesses, all the better. But to even realize that situation, government must give careful consideration to needy citizens and must not fall back on the argument that only other institutions are responsible. God's wisdom for government is this: "Speak up for those who cannot speak for themselves."

REFLECTING . . .

- On which side of the welfare debate do you stand? Why?

- Do you agree with the statement that "no one really earns his or her own way entirely"? How might this hold true for you?

ACTING . . .

- Visit with a social worker in your church or community or with a person who receives government assistance. What are their frustrations? What are their needs? How can you help?

"Whatever you did for one of the least of
these brothers of mine, you did for me."

—Matthew 25:40

- 43 -

RESPONSIBILITY OF AND FOR THE POOR

Proverbs 10:4; 13:23; 14:31; Matthew 25:45

Sloth is one cause of poverty, according to one proverb. Nothing could be more true or more important to understand in the battle against poverty.

Lazy hands make a man poor,
but diligent hands bring wealth.

—Proverbs 10:4

Yet we should not make the mistake of asking a single proverb to bear the full weight of God's revelation about poverty. Don't overlook the message of Proverbs 13:23: "A poor man's field may produce abundant food, but injustice sweeps it away."

How many poor people in our society today are working hard in their respective fields, yet end up with very little because crime reduces their property values to nothing and random violence sweeps away their spouses or parents or children? How many of the poor could be producing abundantly but are unable to do so because failing schools have not prepared them for employment?

Now add the wisdom of another proverb: "He who oppresses the poor shows contempt for their Maker, but whoever is kind to the needy honors God" (14:31). Some poor people need to experience the tough love that pushes them to get jobs; true kindness will not encourage slothful adults to continue in their laziness. But be slow to judge! Many needy persons are not unwilling to work; they are not poor because of laziness. This proverb is crystal clear: All oppression of the poor displays contempt for God. Every person bears the high dignity of being created in God's image. The poor also deserve just treatment and kindness.

If we put these three proverbs together, we come up with a remarkable storehouse of wisdom. That wisdom begins with honoring God in true humility; those who live with abundant wealth should not revel in their own achievements. They should give and receive with hearts of thankfulness. That, in turn, will lead them to see others, including the poor, in the same light—as people called to be thankful stewards of God, their Maker. Proper acts of kindness will then follow.

But acts of kindness by themselves are not enough. They must not blind us to the organized and even institutionalized injustice that also causes and aggravates poverty. Genuine kindness will drive us to seek the reversal of unjust laws and social patterns that sweep away the fruits of the poor person's labor. We should not aim to merely act as perpetual dispensers of charity to the needy. We should also aim to overcome injustice that keeps the poor from enjoying the fruits of their own labors.

And this brings us back to the importance of work. The Creator gave us our marching orders in the beginning, including the command to work six days and to rest every seventh. We all need to work—and to work together—diligently. Everyone's dignity is at stake. If we work together, we will be able to rest together in thankfulness on the sabbath.

REFLECTING . . .

- Why do the pithy sayings from Proverbs pack such practical wisdom in so few words?

- Read the book *Restorers of Hope* (Amy Sherman, Crossway Books, 1997), and see how Sherman's stories and admonitions match up with these proverbs.

ACTING . . .

- Check if the needs for day care, transportation, job training, literacy, and so on are being met for the unemployed or under-employed in your community, and become involved in these efforts.

*"Whatever you did not do for one
of the least of these, you did not do for me."*

—Matthew 25:45

- 44 -

WORK OR DON'T EAT!

2 Thessalonians 3:6-15

Workfare is the word used to describe one of the reforms in the U.S. government's administration of welfare assistance. The idea is that people capable of working should be required to work in order to be eligible for certain welfare benefits. Is this what Paul had in mind when he urged the Thessalonian Christians to shun idlers in order to shame them into working?

Notice first that when Paul wrote to the Thessalonian Christians, he was not writing to government authorities. He was not making a public policy proposal but offering an admonition to a local Christian community. "It is wrong," Paul argued, "for able-bodied Christians to burden fellow Christians by not working. The rule should be that anyone who does not work should not be fed by those who do work."

Even though Paul's words were for a select audience, at least two important elements of this biblical instruction bear on public welfare policy. The first comes from Paul's final comment about shaming an idler. The aim was to shame idlers into becoming full participants in the community; it was not to give working people an excuse to turn against idlers as enemies.

Yet do not regard him [the idler] as an enemy,
but warn him as a brother.

—2 Thessalonians 3:15

The second important ingredient in Paul's admonition is his apparent assumption that the chief, if not the only, failure on the part of the idler was a lack of willpower. Such irresponsibility might be corrected by the shunning power of a local community, which could exert moral authority over the life of the deviant person in their fellowship.

What may we learn from this for our day? First, we Christians should reexamine our own fellowships to ask whether we are doing everything possible to restore idlers to work, treating them as brothers and sisters, not as outcasts. Turning away from them altogether in the expectation that someone else (the public or the market) will assume responsibility for them is to disobey Paul's instruction and to create more problems for our fellow citizens.

Second, if it is true that moral discipline needs to be exercised by people who can hold one another personally accountable, then we should do what we can to promote and extend welfare policies which direct government to give greater support to families, churches, schools, and workplaces. (The Charitable Choice Provision of U.S. welfare law is one such policy which supports these primary institutions of personal care and discipline.)

Workfare may sound like Paul's idea, but if it does nothing to recognize the services provided by primary institutions of care, it may lead merely to the making of more welfare enemies. If workfare focuses only on loafers and not on failed schools, irresponsible parents, and unjust governments, then we may make the mistake of shunning the wrong party. Both in our Christian communities and in the larger public square, we should be working to make it possible for all able-bodied people to "earn the bread they eat" (2 Thess. 3:12).

REFLECTING . . .

- Why is it so difficult to warn someone, as a brother or sister, about bad behavior?

- When assuming responsibility to discipline and care for those who seem able to work but do not, what is the best role for each of these to play: family members, a local congregation, friends, a service organization, local government, federal government?

ACTING . . .

- Continue your needs assessment and involvement with support programs for the unemployed or underemployed in your community (see "Acting . . .," meditation 43).

Never tire of doing what is right.

—2 Thessalonians 3:13

- 45 -

THE WISDOM OF A PUBLIC MAN

Job 29:7-25

The book of Job is a masterpiece of mystery and wisdom. How can one justify the righteousness of both God and Job in face of circumstances that cast doubt on the goodness of both? Job, a man of great rectitude, is suddenly overcome by disasters and awful diseases. How can this be reconciled with divine justice? Why should a righteous man suffer, and how can a good and just God allow such suffering to occur?

In the middle of the sad drama, a remarkable political passage draws us deep into Job's reflections on justice. Mired in his misery, Job thinks back on his earlier happy life and longs "for the days when God watched over me" (Job 29:2). Back then, "when I went to the gate of the city and took my seat in the public square, . . . [people] waited for me as for showers and drank in my words as the spring rain" (vv. 7, 23).

"Whoever heard me spoke well of me, and those who saw me commended me, because I rescued the poor who cried for help, and the fatherless who had none to assist him. . . . I put on righteousness as my clothing; justice was my robe and my turban. I was eyes to the blind and feet to the lame. I was a father to the needy; I took up the case of the stranger. I broke the fangs of the wicked and snatched the victims from their teeth."

—Job 29:11-12, 14-17

Job does not dream first about his former wealth and ease, wishing for the return of servants and the recovery of his own comfort. No, Job recalls with joy his earlier days of public service. Despite the problem of pain and the unfathomable mystery of why God allows the righteous to suffer, Job wishes he could return to the old life of public law and administration. In that high office Job both experienced and demonstrated part of what it means to be created in the image of God by exercising his authority to serve the poor and helpless with wisdom and justice. What a testimony!

The administration of justice in our day is conducted in a very different social context than Job's. Judges presiding in family courts and police tracking down white-collar criminals do not look like Job sitting in the city gate. Yet the task is the same: to protect the innocent and to overcome injustice.

REFLECTING . . .

- What public office today would be responsible for "breaking the fangs of the wicked"? For taking up the "cause of the stranger"?

- Read Jeremiah 22:1-17, and compare it with Job 29. What is the particular reason for public officials to take up the cause of the fatherless and the poor? What did this mean in that ancient context and what might be a comparable meaning in today's context?

ACTING . . .

- If you are not already doing so, become involved in a caring or justice ministry such as Habitat for Humanity, hospice, Meals on Wheels, prison ministry, pro bono legal counseling, or public policy advocacy.

"The man who was dying blessed me;
I made the widow's heart sing."

—Job 29:13

JUSTICE ASSURED

Therefore, holy brothers [and sisters], who share in the heavenly calling, fix your thoughts on Jesus, the apostle and high priest whom we confess. He was faithful to the one who appointed him, just as Moses was faithful in all God's house. Jesus has been found worthy of greater honor than Moses, just as the builder of a house has greater honor than the house itself. For every house is built by someone, but God is the builder of everything. Moses was faithful as a servant in all God's house, testifying to what would be said in the future. But Christ is faithful as a son over God's house. And we are his house, if we hold on to our courage and the hope of which we boast.

—Hebrews 3:1-6

T he sinfully distorted creation has not yet been fully rectified. God, the builder of everything, has not yet finished the house of eternal dwelling. But the fact that the house is being built and will be completed is certain. God, in Christ, by the power of the Holy Spirit, has sealed the promise with blood—the blood of Jesus himself. Justice is assured. Consequently, from now until all things are completed, our human calling is to live and do all our work with courage and hope, confident that the creation will be fulfilled, that God will do justice to everyone and everything.

Hope and Certainty

Living by hope does not mean hoping for something disconnected from our present existence. Paul and the author of Hebrews do not speak of hope for another world but of hope for the fulfillment of this creation. God is building a house composed of human beings who, right now, are being fashioned into the divine dwelling place. The Spirit of God, says Paul, is already at work in us producing the first-fruits of divine indwelling. Right now we are to labor, just as Moses did, as servants in God's house, and we should pray as Moses did that God will "establish the work of our hands" (Ps. 90:17).

---

*We ourselves, who have the firstfruits of the
Spirit, groan inwardly as we wait eagerly for our
adoption as sons, the redemption of our bodies.
For in this hope we were saved. But hope that is
seen is no hope at all. Who hopes for what he
already has? But if we hope for what we do not
yet have, we wait for it patiently.*

—Romans 8:23-25

Our labors in faith now make our hope sure; our diligence through
hope here and now is the means whereby we inherit what has been
promised. Our works do not earn our salvation, as if they could serve
as an acceptable sacrifice for sin. But Christ's blood sacrifice that
washes away sin and makes us acceptable to God does restore us to a
life of service to God. In Christ, we are called back to responsibility in
God's house so that we may make our hope sure. In this respect, our
lives of faith and patience in Christ will inherit what that great
Shepherd has promised for those who belong to him. The Father will
not forget our work and love, but will bring our deeds to fulfillment
through Jesus Christ.

---

*God is not unjust; he will not forget your work and
the love you have shown him as you have helped his
people and continue to help them. We want each of
you to show this same diligence to the very end, in
order to make your hope sure. We do not want you
to become lazy, but to imitate those who through
faith and patience inherit what has been promised.*

—Hebrews 6:10-12

The creation now groans, longing for justice and redemption. The
cause of the groaning is not just the weight of our sin, but also the
Spirit-inspired longing for fulfillment. The Spirit of God is already at
work ahead of time, exposing sin and building up the faithful in
Christ. This is why we know that justice has been secured.

The Trial Date Has Been Set

Justice is assured because God has raised Jesus Christ from the dead, and Christ is the one who will judge the world with justice. So now is the time, during God's restraint of judgment, to repent and join the body that is being fashioned into God's house. After God has pronounced the final sentence, justice will no longer be restrained.

"In the past God overlooked such ignorance, but now he commands all people everywhere to repent. For he has set a day when he will judge the world with justice by the man he has appointed. He has given proof of this to all men by raising him from the dead."

—Acts 17:30-31

We can also be sure of at least two other things: first, that God loves the creation, and second, that throughout history, until the final revelation of God's glory, we will experience the struggle between sin and grace, between hopelessness and hopefulness, between the love of things that lead astray and the love of God that leads to eternal life. The conflict between God's love for creation in Christ, on the one hand, and the sinfulness that stands against Christ, on the other hand, rages even now. That conflict of spirits grips every aspect of life in this age.

The conflict between God and the evil one certainly grips political life. Not that politics is unique in this respect, because the struggle between the true God and false gods ranges over the entire creation. The way the conflict manifests itself in political life is in the struggle between justice and injustice in the life of nations, between well-ordered civic communities and communities torn by strife where governments fail to protect the innocent. Public justice is now assured because God has set a day for Jesus Christ to judge the world. But because Christ has not yet completed his triumph over evil, we still see darkness and distortion on all sides.

That is why our lives of faith and hope in Christ must include standing for justice and fighting against injustice in the political arena here and now. The more we see clearly that the day of final judgment and glory is approaching, the more we should spur one another on to love and good deeds, including the good deeds of public justice (Heb. 10:24-25).

Political Wisdom

To be assured of divine justice not only strengthens hope, it also opens hearts and minds to the wisdom needed for life in this age of conflict. The elementary teachings about Christ are, like milk, essential for infants in the faith, but the author of Hebrews urges believers to mature beyond milk-drinking to the eating of solid food.

But solid food is for the mature, who by constant use have trained themselves to distinguish good from evil.

—Hebrews 5:14

Solid food is necessary for life in this age. Learning to distinguish good from evil is a requirement for politics and government, not just for personal life. Political wisdom, we might say, is one of the fruits of Christian maturity whereby communities of believers learn to distinguish good from evil in public policies, in candidates for office, in the means of resolving conflict, and in cases brought before the public courts.

Political wisdom, built on the confidence that God is establishing justice, makes it possible to distinguish the tasks properly belonging to government from those which belong to churches, families, schools, and other institutions and organizations. The creation, ordained for God's glory, is at stake, and mature Christians must seek to do justice to the manifold diversity of the creation at this moment in history. Sin distorts the world as it now exists, but God's love for creation in Christ removes all excuses for continuing in sin and ignorance.

Amy Sherman, in her book *Restorers of Hope* (Crossway Books, 1997), identifies examples of loving Christian organizations— *restorers*—"dedicated to reaching out to broken people and broken places with a message of hope." *Restorers* know that without the assurance of God's redeeming love, economic incentives, job training, addiction counseling, and motivational therapy are not enough in themselves to restore hope to those who are down and out. *Restorers* have something to teach us, says Sherman, "about how to reinvigorate civil society. Their holistic, rationally based strategy can be a catalyst to spark the increased civic conscientiousness among churchgoers that must accompany a viable shift of welfare responsibilities from the state to society."

As the apostle John reminds us in Revelation, we may not wait until later to act. The Lord is coming soon! The Alpha and the Omega will rectify and fulfill all things. The justice God requires will finally be meted out—to everyone "according to what he has done" (Rev. 22:12). Degrees of justice that have been administered piecemeal throughout this age of conflict will finally be drawn together in the fullness of the kingdom of God. The justice that God presently holds back will one day rush like an unrestrained flood to fill the earth. The justice of God is assured, for God has raised Jesus Christ from the dead and set a day for him to judge the world with justice.

"Behold, I am coming soon! My reward is with me, and I will give to everyone according to what he has done. I am the Alpha and the Omega, the First and the Last, the Beginning and the End."

—Revelation 22:12-13

REFLECTING . . .

- Recall an occasion when you or someone you know took unusual steps to do justice or overcome injustice in a personal or public setting. What motivated the action? Did hope, rooted in Christ's assurance of justice, have anything to do with it?

- Hopelessness is often the most crippling force at work in those hooked into poverty or crime. What are the most important, concrete ways Christians, motivated by hope in Christ, can try to meet the needs of the hopeless?

- People often become discouraged and even cynical when misplaced hope fails. Which recent political movement or legislative enactment do you think manifests a misplaced hope? Why?

ACTING . . .

- Work with others in your church or community to bring love and hope to the hopeless—those in prison, those in addiction programs, the homeless. Even young children can participate in the Angel Tree ministry to prisoners' families or collect food for a food panty or soup kitchen.

JUSTICE HAPPENING

In 1994, Isabel Carter worked for the Tear Fund, a development organization in the United Kingdom. While travelling through Africa, she had a vision of the continent shackled in chains—chains of debt, corruption, hunger, and war. Many in Africa were calling for an end to the burdensome debt. As early as 1990, the All-African Council of Churches called for a Year of Jubilee to cancel Africa's debt, but few in the developed world were listening.

Isabel envisioned the chains breaking, allowing those who were imprisoned to go free. Imagine, she thought, standing against the world's most powerful financial institutions and governments to proclaim that now is the time to break the chains of debt that enslave. She prayed for one encourager to confirm her vision. She continued her travels around Africa, waiting for affirmation of her vision. At the end of one conference, a man approached her and said, "I want you to know that I will do whatever I can do to support your vision."

Thus, a worldwide movement of people and faith was born. *Jubilee 2000—Break the Chains of Debt* is a call to cancel the unpayable debt of the world's poorest countries. In June 1999, ten thousand people formed a human chain in Edinburgh, Scotland. The next day, fifty thousand formed a human chain around the river Thames. Six days later, another fifty thousand formed human chains in Cologne and Stuttgaart, Germany. That same day, a petition with seventeen million signatures gathered from around the world was presented to the International Monetary Fund and the World Bank. The result of all this? World leaders in industrialized countries are canceling debts.

Isabel is like the neighbor who notices a house on fire. Those who have the power to actually fight the blaze are oblivious to its danger until someone sounds the alarm. Isabel's vision and the chain of human support served as the alarm to call the attention of world leaders to the consuming power of debt.

Isabel's story teaches us that sometimes all we have to do is pull the alarm. The unnamed encourager teaches us that encouragement is also a ministry of justice. God will provide the vision and everything we need to assure justice.

MEDITATIONS 46-60

- 46 -

WISDOM AND JUSTICE

Proverbs 29; Romans 13:1-7; 1 Corinthians 2:6-16

Visionary leaders acting righteously and wisely—that's what this country needs. Many of the proverbs speak of such truth.

By justice a king gives a country stability,
but one who is greedy for bribes tears it down.

The righteous care about justice for the poor,
but the wicked have no such concern.

—Proverbs 29:4, 7

All who share political society owe something to one another, and we who enjoy the stability of an enduring constitution and representative government should be even more conscious of how much we owe our children. We owe it to our neighbors to practice justice and exercise wise political stewardship.

The apostle Paul did not discount such wisdom. In fact, if the Roman authorities had spent more time listening to him, they might have learned a great deal from this Jewish scholar of the law who firmly believed that God establishes government for people's good (Rom. 13:1-7). But God gave Paul a further revelation that produced in him even greater wisdom.

The new covenant of which Paul spoke is not one that human beings can renew among themselves merely by deciding to make certain political commitments or by electing wise leaders and adopting better policies. All of this is necessary for citizens to do. But Paul spoke of something larger.

The Spirit of God revealed to Paul the cosmic political implications of the death, resurrection, and ascension of Jesus Christ, implications that encompass the whole creation, including every earthly political society. Now that God has been revealed in the flesh, the beginning of wisdom for any citizen or government official must be to realize that God's wisdom for this world in Christ transcends all other wisdom. Quoting Isaiah, Paul writes, "'No eye has seen, no ear has heard, no mind has conceived what God has prepared for those who love him'—but God has revealed it to us by his Spirit" (1 Cor. 2:9-10).

Accepting Paul's report and admonition as a revelation from God in no way releases new-covenant believers from their civic responsibilities in this age. Rather, the wisdom of God's new covenant now illumines with the brightest of lights the wider context of God's justice and mercy—his judgments and blessings—directed to the entire creation, to every nation, every authority, and all generations.

Jesus Christ has come and is coming to establish justice for the whole world, and he will give more than we can ever imagine to those who trust him. All earthly covenants and constitutions must now be judged in the light of God's final covenant with creation.

REFLECTING . . .

- How does Paul's New Testament message connect God's revelation in Jesus Christ with the wisdom literature of these two Old Testament proverbs?

- Among the unwise, unjust reactions to biblical revelation have been movements such as revolutionary Marxism, Nazism, and utopian democratism that have promised to create a final kingdom of peace on earth. Read a novel or a historical work that illumines the modern humanist quest for alternatives to the kingdom of God.

ACTING . . .

- The next time you watch a fireworks display celebrating an "enduring constitution and representative government," think of Isaiah's words "no eye has seen. . . ." Wonder with your family what God's new creation will be like. Imagine Christ's kingdom when justice is fulfilled.

It is from the LORD that man gets justice.

—Proverbs 29:26

- 47 -

DON'T GIVE UP MEETING TOGETHER

Hebrews 10:19-25

The Christian's hope is based on the historical work of Jesus Christ who opened "a new and living way" for those who follow him. The letter to the Hebrews explains this in great detail and points to implications for our present lives. The great Day toward which we are moving—the Day of God's certain judgment and final redemption of the creation—pulls everyone and everything toward that destiny. Therefore, says the author, act in accord with what you know is coming.

What kind of action should flow from the anticipation of that Day? Should we try to grab all we can while this age lasts—more wealth, more power, and more protection from thieves who break in and steal? Or should we flee this world in spirit and direct our attention to a future world of peace, of golden streets, and of souls freed from bodily limits? Both of these are mistakes, according to Hebrews.

Instead, the writer says, the vision of the "approaching Day" should drive us to "spur one another on toward love and good deeds" (Heb. 10:24). The closer the Day comes to us, the more intense should be our earthly efforts to love one another and to care for our neighbors. This is the time to give, not to be preoccupied with getting. The great and final Day, you see, will come as the bursting, blossoming fulfillment of this day, in blessing and also in judgment. Love and good deeds always have a future.

But how can we spur one another on to love and good deeds in keeping with our hope in Christ? Can each soul-filled body do it alone? Are deeds of love nothing more than isolated acts of individual charity? Of course not! Spurring one another on to love and good deeds requires constant meeting together, constant cooperation, and sometimes even organizing.

---

*Let us not give up meeting together, as some are
in the habit of doing, but let us encourage
one another—and all the more as you see
the Day approaching."*

—Hebrews 10:25

Christians everywhere in the world need to lock arms, to encourage one another. In many places, workers need Christian labor associations through which to organize their relations to fellow workers, managers, and consumers. Christians living in big cities may need to organize urban congresses and neighborhood associations. Christian citizens need to build organizations to assist them in working for public justice.

Certainly meeting together regularly means meeting for worship, gathering as the church on Sunday. However, the author is not talking only about regular worship meetings. No, the accent is on the *act* of meeting, of gathering for the purpose of encouraging one another, of spurring one another on to love and good deeds in all of life. The great Day is coming. Faithfulness requires the entire body of Christ to offer up the whole of life to God in service.

REFLECTING . . .

- Are you hesitant to think that this passage of Scripture may encourage Christians to organize for political service? Why?

- Think of examples in your community of how people working together multiplied love and good deeds. Would the same results have happened if the people involved had worked alone?

ACTING . . .

- Join or give financial support to a Christian organization that works to serve others. Invite others to participate with you.

Let us hold unswervingly to the hope we profess,
for he who promised is faithful.

—Hebrews 10:23

- 48 -

CAN HUMILITY EXIST IN A DEMOCRACY?

Psalm 119:153-168

God and politics? Oh no, not again!

Many Christians are hesitant to talk about obeying God's laws in political life. And rightly so, because such talk can sound like an appeal for imperial or theocratic government. If we start talking about God's will for political life, then before long we may develop strategies for imposing a creed by force or launching a crusade against unbelievers. By and large Christians have accepted secular democracy, agreeing to keep religion to the side and to participate as citizens in a "rational" way without arguing over divine law.

The result of not talking about God's laws for public life, however, is that we learn to accept a system that has little room for humility before the law and little interest in the search for justice. In fact, what now controls politics in North America is interest-group competition. As a consequence, it's becoming increasingly difficult for Christians to humble themselves before laws and governments that seem to represent nothing more than an opponent's victory in the last election. Rather than submit in humility, we gear up our interest groups to beat the incumbent in the next round so we can satisfy our own interests.

Psalm 119 shows us something quite different. The words come from a humble man praising, even thirsting for, God's law. He knows that lawlessness and evil lead to persecution and suffering. He realizes that only God's statutes can renew life and give peace. The spirit of his poetry is joy and thankfulness before God. He wants to submit himself to God's justice.

---

*Seven times a day I praise you for your righteous
laws. Great peace have they who love your law,
and nothing can make them stumble.*

—Psalm 119:164-165

Yet nothing in this psalm implies that humility before divine law requires an imperial or theocratic form of human government. Governments themselves should be humble before God. Moreover, they are not the only authorities called to obey God's law. Parents, entrepreneurs, scientists, artists, doctors, teachers, and many others have a responsibility to seek out and follow divine precepts in their areas of competence. Government, from a biblical point of view, should act humbly as one among many limited authorities before the face of God. Only God has the right to be theocratic.

Christians need a new thirst for the health of God's words, for the truth of God's commands. The spirit of democracy does not always encourage people to submit humbly to God. Yet only through humble submission to God will we be able to learn more about God's will for a just nation as well as for our personal lives. Humility will allow us to play a more responsible role as servants of other people in this country and in countries around the world.

REFLECTING . . .

- Why do people, including Christians, often fear those who appeal to divine law or God's will for politics?

- What evidence do you see of Christian interest groups falling prey to interest-group competition? Can Christian groups play an effective role and still remain humble?

ACTING . . .

- Before you join the cause of a particular interest group or support a candidate for office, consider carefully if that group or candidate acts humbly before God.

Rulers persecute me without cause,
but my heart trembles at your word.

—Psalm 119:161

- 49 -

LABOR FOR THE LORD

Proverbs 6:6, 8; 22:2; 28:3; Deuteronomy 8

As Labor Day rolled around this year, God's Word reminded me again about the importance of work: "Go to the ant, you sluggard . . . consider its ways . . . it stores its provisions in summer and gathers its food at harvest" (Prov. 6:6, 8). At the time, I was also in the middle of reading about Filipino workers who labor 12 to 14 hours a day for only a dollar, and about the extreme poverty in Africa where many people cannot even find work in parched fields and dying villages.

In that state of mind, I recalled a number of other proverbs that reminded me of the constant refrain in Exodus and Deuteronomy that the Lord is the master and owner of all. Deuteronomy 8 is a beautiful summary of how God saved the people of Israel from slavery in Egypt and set them free in a rich, new land where they would have plenty of work and plenty of food so that all could serve one another in humility, knowing that the Lord is master of them all. This is why Israel was to remain distinct from other nations and to serve God only.

Rich and poor have this in common: The LORD is the Maker of them all. . . . A ruler who oppresses the poor is like a driving rain that leaves no crops.

—Proverbs 22:2; 28:3

Grievous problems in many of our jobs today are rooted in attitudes and institutions built on the pure self-interests of owners, managers, or laborers, each pitted against the other. In one case, the diligent work of an entrepreneur may be destroyed by selfish, slothful employees who want much in exchange for little. In another case, a laborer may give more than enough hard work to deserve a good return but the unjust company sweeps it away. Public laws may offer too little encouragement for joint ownership or cooperation between laborers and managers. Soon forgotten is the fear of the God who owns everything. Christians begin to act like everyone else and no longer distinguish themselves as servants of God, as laborers in Christ's kingdom.

The poor can suffer oppression in many ways—not only by unjust employers but by laborers in another country who insist on special protections for their own labor without regard to laborers in other countries. The "oppressor" might be a public law that grants an unfair advantage to certain kinds of labor practices. Whatever the reason, the oppressed always experience the consequence as "a driving rain that leaves no crops."

If you have meaningful work, as I do, give thanks to God for a very rich blessing. And together, let's work for justice that will help to lift the yoke of oppression from all those laborers, owners, managers, and unemployed people who do not know the joy of serving the Lord freely with their hands.

REFLECTING . . .

- Do you like the work you do? What is just and unjust about the conditions under which you work?

- Would you be willing to change your consumer practices if you knew unfair labor laws or poor working conditions existed in the place where these goods were produced? How can you find out?

ACTING . . .

- Investigate the tax laws, safety regulations, and so on that govern the profit-making or non-profit organization for which you or other family members work. Make a list of all the laws that seem good and all that seem to be a nuisance or unnecessary red tape. Talk with management to see their perspective, and work together to initiate changes where possible. (If you're an employer, encourage this dialogue with your employees.)

But remember the LORD your God, for it is
he who gives you the ability to produce wealth.

—Deuteronomy 8:18

- 50 -

TO SERVE HIM IN ALL OUR WAYS

Romans 12:9-21

If ever there was a concentrated, forceful admonition to serve our neighbors with humility and without reservation, it can be found in Paul's letter to the Romans. Honor others above yourself. Never give up loving. Bless those who persecute you. Don't be proud. Feed the hungry. Don't take revenge. On and on Paul goes, relentlessly driving home the message of Christian service in love.

Never be lacking in zeal, but keep
your spiritual fervor, serving the Lord.

—Romans 12:11

How can we practice what Paul preaches? Christians often try their best, whether at home or on the job, to be nice to their immediate neighbors. Conscientious Christians may also spend time repenting of evil thoughts about a nasty coworker or of hateful words spoken behind someone's back.

But what is frequently missing from such personal conscientious-ness is a wider awareness of the actions that institutions and organizations take in structuring our lives and our neighbors' lives. Most of us don't control big governments or big businesses, so we don't often think about our responsibility for society. Yet we have been called as God's people and given a shared obligation to serve our neighbors through the organizations and institutions in which we jointly participate.

Paul's letter to the Roman Christians wasn't written for lone individuals to read in isolation, but for all the saints in Rome to read and act on in community. Christians as a body must follow a course different from the courses followed by groups and institutions whose first principles are pride, impatience, self-congratulation, envy, and self-preservation.

You and I may think we are sincere and conscientious individuals, but what kind of citizens are we? Can we support the way city, state, and federal governments structure the lives of our neighbors? Do the companies from which we buy goods and services and for which we work carry on their business for the health and benefit of all our neighbors? Do our churches mourn with those who mourn and associate with people of low position?

Through Paul's letter to the Romans, God calls us to something different from personal piety with social blinders. He commands us, through grace and rebirth in Christ, to serve him in all our ways by serving all our neighbors in all avenues of life.

In fact, these verses at the end of Romans 12 introduce Paul's instructions about the meaning of politics in Romans 13. God has established government to be a servant—an expression of the very service that we should render to our neighbors. Government bears a communal responsibility before God.

REFLECTING . . .

- Read Romans 12 and 13 as though all of the admonitions are addressed to *you* in the plural, rather than in the singular. What difference does this make in your understanding of Paul's words?

- How would you rate your church in terms of carrying out the instructions Paul gives? What changes would make your neighbors recognize your church as a haven of God's love?

ACTING . . .

- At your place of work or with a group of friends, organize a discussion group to explore what the Bible says about shared obligations to serve your neighbors. Each time you meet, listen to the Bible speak to *us* and *you* (plural) with a call to action.

Be devoted to one another in brotherly love. . . .
If it is possible, as far as it depends on you,
live at peace with everyone.

—Romans 12:10, 18

- 51 -
FOOD SCARCITY OR POPULATION GLUT?

Exodus 1:8-22; Deuteronomy 27:17; Amos 5:9-11; Isaiah 5:8

Roelf Haan, a Dutch economist who worked for years in Buenos Aires, Argentina, says this about contemporary land ownership, food production, and population growth:

> There are those who say that the world hunger problem has reached such vast proportions that we can only go at it by offering a policy of free play to the prevailing economic and political powers, to the multinational corporations and "no-nonsense" governments. But this bypasses the origins of the drama. In our economic system, increasing agricultural production does not necessarily mean that the poor will be favoured or that justice and agriculture will be promoted. In the third world, agriculture is more and more geared to export—to benefit meat production in the overfed West and the manufacture of alcoholic drinks and articles of luxury . . . and other industrial goods.
>
> Whenever the poor are driven out of their land in order to advance the power system, as we see happening in the "model" villages in Guatemala and the Philippines, we may see agricultural production taking place, but there is no land development to benefit those who live there.
>
> The Bible allows no misunderstanding about [land ownership]. "Cursed be he who removes his neighbor's landmark" (Deut. 27:17, RSV). And the prophet Amos pronounces judgment over those who trample down the lowly and hate those who speak up for justice and who force the poor peasants to make exorbitant payments in wheat (5:9-11).

—Roelf Haan, *The Economics of Honour:
Biblical Reflections on Money and Property*
(WCC Publications, World Council of Churches, 1988).

---

*Woe to those who join house to house, who add field
to field, until there is no more room, and you are
made to dwell alone in the midst of the land.*

—Isaiah 5:8 (RSV)

159

We are often told of a world *population* problem to divert attention from the world *food* problem and the widespread necessity of *land reform*. But that myth about the "too great a world population" can be easily exposed.

The argument runs that the population is becoming unsustainable because of the demands on natural resources, energy, and environment which a newborn baby on an average world scale will make throughout his or her lifetime. *But the demands of the average newborn baby are not the problem.* The excessive use of energy comes not from the baby born in Bolivia but from the baby born in the Netherlands or the United States.

We don't need a "politics of population" as much as a politics of food and land distribution; not the policy of the Pharaoh in Egypt who felt threatened by the demographic growth of the Israelites, whom he was exploiting economically, but a policy of development in which legal aid and land reform are central. Only when the "countryland" blossoms will it be apparent how much room the city is entitled to. Only when the needs of the poorest stand first will it be apparent how far we can look into the interests of the wealthy.

REFLECTING . . .

- What kind of economic growth would most help the poor in America and other parts of the world today?

- Invite to your home or church education class four or five fellow Christians, each of whom works in a different sector of the economy (banking, agriculture, commerce, industry, a non-profit organization, government, and so forth). Discuss the relationships that tie them together. In what respects do poor people suffer as a result of our current economic system? In what respects do they benefit?

ACTING . . .

- Contribute financially or in some other tangible way to organizations such as Bread for the World. Encourage others in your church or community to join you in this effort.

> *"Look, [said Pharaoh,] the Israelites have*
> *become much too numerous for us."*
>
> —Exodus 1:9

- 52 -

IDENTIFYING WITH WHAT ENDURES

Psalm 119:49-56, 89-96, 137-152

That someone would express personal identification with God's commandments in a typical American news broadcast, TV sitcom, or popular magazine article is almost inconceivable. On the other hand, we're not at all surprised to find people identifying themselves with fast cars, sleek boats, smooth liquors, and fat bank accounts.

But which is more enduring and closest to the center of human identity? Is it the possessions we have or God's will for life? Is it more realistic to believe that the next president and Congress will secure our prosperity once and for all or that God's promises will last forever? Is it smarter to trust that one's Wall Street investments will guarantee a happy future or to look for enduring comfort in God's words?

The psalmist has no doubt about the correct answer. This is not piety repressing libido or romantic idealism ignoring reality. The psalmist confronts reality, speaking for both himself and the downtrodden.

---

*My comfort in my suffering is this: Your promise
preserves my life. . . . Indignation grips me because
of the wicked, who have forsaken your law.
Your decrees are the theme of my song
wherever I lodge. . . . My zeal wears me out,
for my enemies ignore your words.*

—Psalm 119:50, 53-54, 139

Contemporary culture encourages us to treat as real only that which we have in hand or see immediately before our eyes. Modern or postmodern people cannot identify their lives with God's commandments. Yet the consequence is that people, and not just the products of our hands, become utterly disposable. Nothing has depth or lasting significance.

Because God created humans to be inventive, when we forget God we begin to imagine that we can create our own lives. We think of ourselves, our wishes, our imaginations as the law of life. The mark of modernity is to believe that humans are autonomous. Instead of meditating on God's law day and night in order to gain direction for our inventiveness, we meditate on our own wishes and desires and then spend our days trying to make reality fit our plans. The outcome is death.

But if human life is truly worthwhile, then its depth and integrity must be rediscovered in what endures—in the communion, love, and hope that open hearts, enlarge minds, and widen the scope of human fellowship. An utterly realistic psalmist pointed the way to recovery a long time ago: "To all perfection I see a limit; but your commands are boundless" (Ps. 119:96).

REFLECTING . . .

- When you hear of meditating on God's law, is your first reaction to think of legalism or to think of life? Why?

- List a few of the things about life that you would most like to see endure forever. What, if anything, do they have to do with God's precepts and promises?

ACTING . . .

- Attempt in some way this week to "widen the scope of human fellowship" by reaching out to someone who has been treated as "disposable" by society. Pray particularly for those in pubic office who should be administering laws in ways that uphold the dignity of each person.

Your promises have been thoroughly tested,
and your servant loves them.

—Psalm 119:140

- 53 -

How Long Will Evil Prosper?

Proverbs 21:30

Proverbs 21 gives us a simple statement without temporal qualification.

There is no wisdom, no insight,
no plan that can succeed against the Lord.

—Proverbs 21:30

But it can't be true," you say. "Just look around. Are not the insights and plans of drug dealers, pornographers, loan sharks, and gambling casino owners succeeding quite well?"

Should we conclude, as many do, that the presence of so much evil in this world proves that God is evil, since God allows it to happen? Or do we say there is no God, because a loving God would not permit evil?

To be sure, there is no simple answer to this dilemma. Evil surrounds us and all too often appears to be succeeding. But perhaps we fail to recall how many human plans have already failed in the course of history. Perhaps we give too much weight to the temporary influence of insights that oppose the Lord, while giving too little weight to their rapid decline in case after case, in fad after fad. Do we get so caught up in jumping from one temporary wisdom to another that we fail to grasp the wisdom of the Lord?

Consider these historical happenings: slavery is now anathema; Hitler's very name stands for an utterly disreputable form of politics; the Soviet Union has collapsed; China is rejecting old ways of economic totalitarianism; the international drug cartel, which once thrived in secret, now stands exposed. Doesn't history confirm the proverb's judgment after all?

"Yes," you say, "but for every evil exposed and for every foolish fad that evaporates, two or three new ones take their place." The whole world sometimes looks like my friend Ivan Romero's description of Panama—a disaster beyond crisis which is headed for catastrophe. Indeed, this is precisely when a sense of timing is most important.

The proverb does not say that opposition will not arise; it says only that it cannot succeed against the Lord.

A genuinely hopeful perspective on the times in which we live cannot be manufactured by putting on rose-colored glasses to disguise evil. Too many deaths, broken lives, and broken hearts flow from our multiple plans and insights for us to pretend that evil does not surround us. Hopefulness is rooted in the certainty of the Lord's victory against all opposition, not in wishful thinking. Seeking out and following the paths of the Lord's wisdom will not allow us to cover up evil in a fit of optimism. Instead, the Lord exposes evil for what it is—the God-defying, human-degrading actions and tendencies that cannot finally succeed.

What will succeed? Obedience to the Lord in all things. That alone. Even when obedience must be pursued in face of evil powers that temporarily appear to be winning, even when obedience leads to death on a cross, the Lord will succeed in overcoming everything that stands in opposition.

REFLECTING . . .

- What event in your life has most strongly renewed your sense of assurance that the Lord will not let injustice endure forever?

- Christian organizations working to end substance abuse, abortion, environmental degradation, or world hunger often face discouraging obstacles. What do you think keeps them going? (If possible, invite representatives of these organizations to share their work and insights with your group.)

ACTING . . .

- Become a prayer or financial partner to one of the organizations you identified.

A false witness will perish, and whoever
listens to him will be destroyed forever.

—Proverbs 21:28

- 54 -
HAVE NOTHING TO DO WITH THEM!
2 Timothy 3

In an essay written after the fall of communism in Eastern Europe, Vaclav Havel, now president of the Czech Republic, commented on the pressures he felt in public office after the "easy" part of the revolution was over. Despite agonizing difficulties, he remained "deeply convinced that politics is not essentially a disreputable business." But the only way forward is "to live in truth" (*The New York Review of Books*, April 9, 1992).

Politics is an art different from writing plays or conducting a business venture or parenting children. Each must be pursued in keeping with its own distinctive character. Yet, as Havel suggests, it's amazing to discover how important certain basic human virtues are in the pursuit of every human activity, including "high politics." Havel "discovered that good taste is more important than a postgraduate degree in political science. . . . Qualities like fellow-feeling, the ability to talk to others, insight, the capacity to grasp quickly not only problems but also human character, the ability to make contact, a sense of moderation—all these are immensely more important in politics."

In this context, compare the apostle Paul's admonition to young Timothy after he entered the high office of pastor and elder in the early church. The aim of God's people is to "make contact" with everyone, to display the character of godliness, to exhibit "fellow-feeling" and "insight" so that all might come to the knowledge of God revealed in Christ Jesus.

In order to be equipped for every good work, Timothy needed to learn from those whose habits were good and to avoid those whose habits were destructive. Timothy, like the rest of us, had to learn to live at peace with all people insofar as it was in his power to do so. Yet learning to be tolerant and open to others does not mean picking up the habits of everybody one meets.

But mark this: There will be terrible times in the last days. People will be lovers of themselves, lovers of money, boastful, proud, abusive, disobedient to their parents, ungrateful, unholy, without love, unforgiving, slanderous, without self-control, brutal,

not lovers of the good, treacherous, rash, conceited,
lovers of pleasure rather than lovers of God—having
a form of godliness but denying its power.

—2 Timothy 3:1-5

Some people exhibit very bad taste, indeed, whether they are communists or capitalists, totalitarians or democrats. They cannot possibly be living in the truth. They may have postgraduate degrees and long experience on the job. "But," says Paul, "my advice is unequivocal: Have nothing to do with them." Paul's admonition is not that Timothy should hide from the world; rather, it is that he should live by the right principles in the world while having nothing to do with those who insist on corrupting God's good creation, which is now assured of a just trial in the Lord's court.

REFLECTING . . .

- Why are those who try to separate themselves from evildoers often called self-righteous or sectarian? Is there any justification for these charges? How should Christians go about separating themselves?

- Think of a very personal and a very political example of slander or brutality or rashness. How would you act to "hate the sin while loving the sinner?"

ACTING . . .

- The next time you vote, weigh carefully which candidates defy the character traits Paul describes (vv. 2-3). Keep separate from those who do evil, and pray vigorously for those who want to do right.

Everyone who wants to live a godly
life in Christ Jesus will be persecuted.

—2 Timothy 3:12

- 55 -

PROSPERITY OR HUNGER—
WHICH IS BEST?

Deuteronomy 8:1-20

Prosperity or hunger—which is best? An absurd question. Who would ever vote for hunger if prosperity is an option?

But what if short-term hunger could lead to sustained prosperity while short-sighted prosperity would lead to tragic disaster? More complicated, isn't it?

At the turn of the millennium, the U.S. economy appears to be extremely strong, yet the country is heavily in debt to the rest of the world. Many Americans enjoy abundant prosperity, but depend on borrowing to keep spending. The kind of prosperity we now have may be little more than an entry way to disaster.

If you add to this consideration the fact that God will have the last word about the false gods we serve, then you realize how unhelpful and illusory prosperity might be. This is exactly what God told Israel when leading them into the promised land, flowing with milk and honey.

> *You may say to yourself, "My power and the strength of my hands have produced this wealth for me." But remember the LORD your God, for it is he who gives you the ability to produce wealth. . . . If you ever forget the LORD your God and follow other gods and worship and bow down to them, I testify against you today that you will surely be destroyed.*

—Deuteronomy 8:17-19

So we're convinced that illegitimate prosperity might lead to ultimate destruction. But how in the world can hunger lead to prosperity?

We've all heard that hard work and discipline are what make savings and prosperity possible. That's what God taught Israel in the wilderness. Moses explained to the people that God "humbled you, causing you to hunger and then feeding you with manna. . . . Know then in your heart that as a man disciplines his son, so the LORD your

God disciplines you" (Deut. 8:3, 5). The point, you see, is that hunger connected with obedience to God's commands can lead to the genuine prosperity of good stewardship in a "good land" (v. 7) where "you will lack nothing" (v. 9).

God does not call us to live without food or to seek hunger. God calls us to feed the hungry and to turn from evil. The question is this: How shall we live now in this age before the face of God in the assurance that justice will be established?

God aims to "teach you that man does not live on bread alone but on every word that comes from the mouth of the LORD" (v. 3). If we seek prosperity on our own terms, we will surely perish. If we hunger for God's Word, we will be filled.

REFLECTING . . .

- What is right and wrong about the so-called "prosperity gospel" (the teaching that following Jesus and being right with God lead to financial and material prosperity)?

- To better understand the "prosperity gospel" preached on TV by Robert Tilton and in many churches today, read Tilton's *God's Laws of Success* (Farmers Branch, Tex.: Robert Tilton Ministries, 1985). Invite others to read and discuss it with you.

ACTING . . .

- Encourage your church family to become involved in a ministry to relieve hunger in your local or global community. To help children become aware of hunger issues, you might want to use the devotional book *With a Cherry on Top* (Carol Reinsma, CRC Publications, 1997).

When you have eaten and are satisfied, praise the
LORD your God for the good land he has given you.

—Deuteronomy 8:10

- 56 -

FREEDOM—NO COVER-UP FOR EVIL

1 Peter 2:13-25; Micah 6:8

Election time! It's more than a time to vote. It's a time to celebrate the great privilege of living in a free society where we can elect our government without coercion. The United States, Canada, and many other countries around the world are free, democratic countries. Rejoice!

Indeed, those of us who live in *free* countries have much for which to give thanks. Political freedom is a rare commodity and should not be taken lightly. But what is freedom for? Why is a free election a privilege? Oftentimes, much campaign rhetoric celebrates freedom as an end in itself. In fact, freedom is elevated to such heights that some say they are willing to go to any extreme to defend it.

Peter teaches something much more modest and humble about the privilege of freedom in a political setting. His words, which include the command to submit to every authority instituted by God, are familiar ones. Political authority is a gift from God and is to be approached with that in mind. True freedom, according to Peter, is not rooted in a political order but in the God who rules over the political world. The chief end of human life is not freedom, but service to God.

Live as free men, but do not use your freedom as a cover-up for evil; live as servants of God.

1 Peter 2:16

From a biblical perspective, government does not exist for the sake of freedom; government exists to do public justice, to punish evil and to reward the good. Public justice in turn makes room for the freedom people need to live responsibly before the face of God, even though many free citizens do not use their freedom for that purpose.

One of the greatest misuses of political freedom in our day is the attempt to cover up evil. Few politicians running for office are interested in telling the whole truth. Often the two pictures presented by competing candidates in an election are incompatible with each other and unrecognizable to the average citizen. Superficiality, half truths, and demagoguery dominate even the mildest campaign speeches. Voters are left with doubts about what a candidate can or will do along with a cynical distaste for the whole political process. The percentage of eligible voters who actually go to the polls in the United States mocks our high-sounding slogans about the privilege of living in a free, democratic country.

If you believe that the Bible has authority over your life, then you had better not sit at ease with the cynics and the "cover-up" politicians who talk so glibly about freedom today. "Silence the ignorant talk of foolish men" (1 Peter 2:15), and begin to live as a truly free person. Don't use your freedom as a cover-up for evil, but live as a thankful servant of God. Seek justice, love mercy, and walk humbly with your God (Micah 6:8).

REFLECTING . . .

• Why does the Bible say that true human freedom is found in being bound as a servant—a bond servant—to God through Jesus Christ?

• If governments are to impose and enforce laws, why do so many political candidates say that they will ease government restrictions? How will this campaign promise influence you in the next election?

ACTING . . .

• Give thanks for the privilege of voting.

---

*Show proper respect to everyone: Love the
brotherhood of believers, fear God, honor the king.*

—1 Peter 2:17

- 57 -

IRANAMOK AND I TOLD YOU SO

John 14:15-31

American media commentators coined the phrase *Iranamok* to describe the Iran-Contra scandal in the 1980s. Others simply said, "I told you so! Politics is like that—people misusing power and going to the dogs. What else can you expect?"

This is a typical response to corruption in high places. For some people, politics is always suspect. Those with power will eventually misuse it.

Quite in contrast to suspicion and cynicism, people also sometimes invest too much hope in politics. They want to believe that a new president or prime minister, a new Congress or Parliament can change the world, end poverty, or stop racism by one program or another. Much of what drives politics, even when the politicians promise to get government off our backs, is wishing for and being promised the moon. Then, of course, when the grandiose hopes don't pan out, people fall back once again into cynicism and hopelessness.

Quite a different "I told you so" comes from Jesus. In fact, it's a present-tense "I'm telling you so."

"All this I have spoken while still with you. But the Counselor, the Holy Spirit, whom the Father will send in my name, will teach you all things. . . . I have told you now before it happens, so that when it does happen you will believe."

—John 14:25-26, 29

But what do Jesus' words have to do with grand hopes and deep cynicism in politics today?

If ever there was a person who could have won a tremendous political following by dishing out big promises, it was Jesus. The miracles Jesus performed far outshone anything that came after him, whether from Napoleon, Lenin, George Washington, or Franklin Roosevelt. The zealots, among others, were willing to follow Jesus to the death to try to rid Israel of Roman rulers.

But Jesus did not exploit his temporary political potential. His Father had bigger plans. Jesus spent his time pointing to God the Father, demonstrating and teaching humility. Jesus didn't promise his followers a short-term political pay-off, but rather the coming presence of the Spirit of God—the Comforter, the Counselor—who would continue to teach the disciples and give them peace for eternity.

Jesus explained ahead of time that the evil one, the prince of this world, would drive him to the cross. All temporary political hopes would be crushed. But in the long run, that prince "has no hold on" Jesus (v. 30). The more important news, which Jesus also told ahead of time, was that the coming Spirit would never leave the disciples and would lead them into all the truths of God's kingdom.

Grounded in the promises of Jesus and led by the true Counselor, we should be neither surprised by Iranamoks nor misled by grandiose political promises. Instead, we should learn the realism, the balance, the patience, and the humility of public service to our King who rules the whole world. Justice is assured! I am telling you so.

REFLECTING . . .

- Why do North Americans seem to have such high expectations from government and yet, at the same time, such cynicism and low regard for it? Do you sense this struggle personally?

- Look up the phrase *kingdom of heaven* or *kingdom of God* in a Bible dictionary. How is Jesus' authority related to the human political authorities of this world? How does this help you understand that a follower of Jesus can be politically responsible in this world?

ACTING . . .

- Especially around an election time, covenant to pray regularly with at least one other Christian. Ask the Spirit to keep you from cynicism, to give you realistic expectations about government, and to comfort you.

"I do not give to you as the world gives. Do not let your hearts be troubled and do not be afraid."

—John 14:27

- 58 -

IMPATIENCE BREEDS IDOLATRY

Exodus 32:1-35; 2 Peter 3:1-13

The story of Israel's construction and worship of a golden calf after
God led the people out of Egypt is a familiar one. Moses had gone up
the mountain to receive God's law for the newly independent nation.
While he was out of sight, the people grew impatient and, with
Aaron's help, turned to idol worship. God was angry. Moses was so
dismayed after descending the mountain that he threw down the
tablets of the covenant and broke them. When Moses confronted
Aaron about the debacle, Aaron made excuses.

---

*"Do not be angry, my lord," Aaron answered. "You
know how prone these people are to evil. They said
to me, 'Make us gods who will go before us. As for
this fellow Moses who brought us up out of Egypt,
we don't know what has happened to him.'"*

—Exodus 32:22-23

When Jesus came, he announced the culmination of God's rule
over the earth. But Christ's announcement required, and still requires, great patience on the part of his followers. This greatly frustrated the Zealots, who thought they had waited long enough for
God to release the chosen people from Roman rule. Not long after
Jesus' resurrection and ascension, people complained much like the
Israelites did. They asked, "Where is this 'coming' he promised?"
(2 Peter 3:4). They wondered what had happened to this Jesus who
had promised to establish God's kingdom. The people longed for
something more visible, more tangible, to give them a sense of
concrete identity under God here and now. In many respects, kings
and rulers, constitutions and flags became the idols that displace
God.

Political order has, from earliest times, been the chief means of
binding people together with a comprehensive sense of identity,
locating them securely in the world with a sense of divine mission.
This is why the Roman Catholic church, Eastern Orthodox church,
and most Protestant churches remained preoccupied for so long with

ordering, or being ordered by, political institutions, whether imperial, feudal, or national.

The people of God today live under many earthly governments yet have been called to honor Christ as their King. This is not much different from the people of Israel, who had earthly governors like Moses, but who were supposed to acknowledge God as their ultimate King. Israel's problem did not arise from Moses' temporary absence, but from their lack of trust in God's kingship.

Impatience that breeds political idolatry continues to produce its bad fruits today. It is well and good for Jesus to rule from on high, many believe, but why doesn't he act more quickly to prove and demonstrate his authority? Peter, recalling God's past judgment of the world by a flood and undoubtedly remembering God's slaughter of 3,000 golden-calf worshipers, says this to the impatient ones: "By the same word the present heavens and earth are reserved for fire, being kept for the day of judgment and destruction of ungodly men" (2 Peter 3:7). God will fulfill all covenant promises. The kingdom will come! As for us today, we must learn godly patience—even in politics.

REFLECTING . . .

- How should we persist patiently, resting in God's assurance that justice will be done, while facing so much injustice in the political world?

- Read the story of the golden calf to a group of children, and ask them to describe as many of its political features as possible. Who is the ultimate ruler? What is Moses' role? Who makes the law? Who acts as the judge?

ACTING . . .

- Put into practice one of the "how-to" ideas suggested in the first reflecting question above.

With the Lord a day is like a thousand years,
and a thousand years are like a day.

—2 Peter 3:8

- 59 -
BOTH LORD AND CHRIST
Psalm 16:8-11; Acts 2:22-36

The apostle Peter's first sermon after Pentecost was an unqualified affirmation of the direct connection between Jesus and justice— between the particularity of the Messiah and the universality of God's kingdom. The great king David was a prophet, said Peter. David foresaw that God would place one of David's descendants on his throne (Ps. 16:8-11). Jesus is the fulfillment of that promise. Jesus is the Christ, the Messiah, the Anointed One.

"Therefore let all Israel be assured of this:
God has made this Jesus, whom you
crucified, both Lord and Christ."

—Acts 2:36

Not everyone accepted Peter's testimony. Many rejected it with hostility. It embarrassed many Jews. Perhaps more of them would have been willing to accept Jesus if he had established God's universal kingdom immediately upon arrival. Many Gentiles who later heard the gospel might also have responded positively in greater numbers if this particular Jew, Jesus, had established a political order of universal justice. What kind of faith does it take to believe in a Messiah, no longer present, who leaves behind nothing but promises and politically powerless disciples?

For most people today, Christian or not, it is relatively easy to say that we want justice to be done. Most Americans say they believe in God—a God who somehow rules over all, even if this divine authority seems fairly remote from the world in which we live day by day. Many Christians believe that when Jesus comes again and actually establishes his universal kingdom, the connection between God and justice will be made. But for now, the connection doesn't really exist.

As I write this, another session of the United States Congress is opening. Looking out over Washington, it sounds odd and even embarrassing to most people working in government for me to say that Jesus is Lord over all earthly authorities, including all elected representatives and presidents. It would be more acceptable, more practical and relevant, to appeal to general, rational principles of justice without looking for a connection between them and Jesus.

But if we are to take seriously the biblical claims of Jesus, then the connection between Jesus and earthly justice cannot be ignored or broken. God's kingdom is not simply future and heavenly; it is unfolding now—both in judgment and in blessing. God's universal standards of justice are not rational abstractions. They hold for this particular creation, which is sustained by the Son of God, through whom all things were created in the first place. Jesus Christ embodies God's universal rule; he is both Lord and Christ!

Through Christ alone are God's universal standards of justice guaranteed.

REFLECTING . . .

- Do you agree that "most people today, Christian or not, . . . want justice to be done"? What evidence do you see in your community to support your response?

- Why do we have difficulty recognizing Christ's political lordship in a democracy where many people do not acknowledge his authority?

ACTING . . .

- Take time to pray, both by yourself and with others, that God will deepen our understanding of this part of the Lord's prayer: "Your will be done on earth as it is in heaven." Think and pray about how we should act on this prayer in a political way.

"God has raised this Jesus to life,
and we are all witnesses of the fact."

—Acts 2:32

- 60 -
ENVISIONING THE NEW ORDER
Hebrews 2:1-18; Psalm 8:4-6

The writer of the letter to the Hebrews had an overwhelming vision of human fulfillment—a vision of a new order that will bring to climax the whole of human history. But the path to fulfillment is littered with human failure and incompetence. The vision seems fraught with internal contradictions. How can human fulfillment be built on the history of human failure?

The author of Hebrews, quoting the psalmist, is convinced beyond doubt that God created human beings to be the crown of the entire creation. But at the same time, history is strewn with human wreckage that does not display glory and honor and fails to care for everything placed under human feet. Nevertheless, the Hebrews writer believes firmly that the movement toward fulfillment is on track.

---

*What is man that you are mindful of him, the son
of man that you care for him? You made him a
little lower than the heavenly beings and crowned
him with glory and honor. You made him ruler
over the works of your hands; you put
everything under his feet.*

—Psalm 8:4-6

How do these three "certainties" hang together? Right now we do not see everything ordered properly under human feet as it should be (Heb. 2:8). "But we see Jesus, who was made a little lower than the angels, now crowned with glory and honor because he suffered death, so that by the grace of God he might taste death for everyone" (v. 9).

The good news that resolves the contradictions of the universe is that God stooped down beneath divine dignity to suffer the judgment deserved by creatures who failed to live up to the honor and glory for which they were created. At present, we do not yet see the glorious fulfillment of human life. But we see Jesus.

However tragic it may seem that Jesus should suffer because of our failure, all the way to the wreckage of death, it was God's will for him to do so. In bringing many children to glory, "it was fitting that God, for whom and through whom everything exists, should make the author of their salvation perfect through suffering. Both the one who makes [people] holy and those who are made holy are of the same family. So Jesus is not ashamed to call them brothers [and sisters]" (vv. 10-11).

The climactic fulfillment of the ages, for which forgiven sinners are destined, will reveal the complete reconciliation between God and the image of God. Justice will not be contradicted. The entire creation will be reordered in perfect righteousness because Jesus became like us "in every way, in order that he might become a merciful and faithful high priest in service to God" (v. 17). The Creator is restoring creation. The Redeemer is reconciling fallen humans to the glory of Jesus Christ.

REFLECTING . . .

- What does it mean politically that God put "everything under human feet"?

- The phrase "we see Jesus" implies seeing by faith, not by ordinary sight. What is the difference between pursuing civic responsibility based on faith in democracy and pursuing it based on faith in Christ? What is the difference between what one *sees* in each case?

ACTING . . .

- Celebrate the worldwide community of faith by occasionally worshiping with a different church family or with Christians from another country. Ask them to describe how they exercise civic responsibility in service to God through Christ.

In putting everything under him,
God left nothing that is not subject to him.

—Hebrews 2:8

JUSTICE FULFILLED

But you have come to Mount Zion, to the heavenly Jerusalem, the city of the living God. You have come to thousands upon thousands of angels in joyful assembly, to the church of the firstborn, whose names are written in heaven. You have come to God, the judge of all men, to the spirits of righteous men made perfect, to Jesus the mediator of a new covenant, and to the sprinkled blood that speaks a better word than the blood of Abel. . . . Therefore, since we are receiving a kingdom that cannot be shaken, let us be thankful, and so worship God acceptably with reverence and awe, for our "God is a consuming fire."

—Hebrews 12:22-24, 28-29

The kingdom that cannot be shaken is the city of the living God—the new Jerusalem—which brings all of God's promises of justice for creation to final realization. From the standpoint of our life in this age, we gather around Mount Zion only through faith and in hopeful anticipation. But, as the Scriptures make clear, our anticipation amounts to much more than mere wishful thinking.

The reality is that Jesus Christ has gone on ahead of us and has already opened the gates of the city. The Holy Spirit's living testimony, among us right now, gives us confidence that we "have come to Mount Zion" (Heb. 12:22), that our elder brother has already entered the new Jerusalem on our behalf. Mount Zion rises before us as reality. Through faith in Christ, the mediator of the new covenant, we may celebrate, in the present tense, the truth that "we are receiving a kingdom that cannot be shaken" (v. 28).

When the awesome judge and "consuming fire" (v. 29) completes the cleansing of creation and the unveiling of the kingdom, we will then know what constitutes perfect justice, what it means to be fully righteous. Yet even now, because of what God has revealed ahead of time, we already know a great deal about justice fulfilled.

Creation Fulfilled

At the very beginning of creation God pronounced satisfaction with "all that he had made" and "blessed the seventh day and made it holy" (Gen. 1:31; 2:1-3). The fulfillment of justice will mean God's complete satisfaction in sabbath joy. Ultimate justice means the creation is fulfilled, with every creature receiving its due.

Psalm 72, one of the many psalms that looks ahead in faith to the completion of God's work, sings of the king who will finally be satisfied because he has established justice. The prophets of Israel, testifying long before Jesus was born, saw expansive visions of God's kingdom fulfilled, both in the sense that all wrongs had been righted through final judgment and in the sense that the creation had received its full reward, measured by God's complete satisfaction.

He will rule from sea to sea and from the
River to the ends of the earth.

The desert tribes will bow before him and his
enemies will lick the dust. . . . All kings will bow
down to him and all nations will serve him.
For he will deliver the needy who cry out,
the afflicted who have no one to help.

—Psalm 72:8-9, 11-12

Marxism, fascism, and various messianic nationalisms have all promised to establish justice once and for all, to bring heaven down to earth. They are secularized distortions of the biblical vision of creation fulfilled. They function as substitute religions and have converted millions of people. Marxism is largely discredited today, but fascist and other nationalistic fervors are very much alive.

In reaction to these secular ideologies of redemption, Christians often emphasize the supernatural other-worldliness of Christ's coming kingdom. Like ancient gnostics, they believe that salvation and final justice will come only when God takes Christians out of this fallen world. Biblical language about a new heaven and a new earth suggests to them that God will start over after destroying the first creation. Yet this picture makes it difficult, if not impossible, to grasp the meaning of God's redemption and fulfillment of the good creation which was made in and for the Son of God.

Christian citizens today need to demonstrate in word and deed that Christ's lordship makes no political room for either substitute messiahs or world-flight escapists. The new heaven and new earth represent the fulfillment of God's creation made possible by the one through whom and for whom all things were created.

Resurrection Justice

The apostle Paul, writing of the resurrected and ascended Jesus, explains that Jesus Christ is the token signifying the guarantee of the resurrection of all God's people.

---

*For as in Adam all die, so in Christ all will be made
alive. But each in his own turn: Christ, the
firstfruits; then, when he comes, those who belong to
him. Then the end will come, when he hands over
the kingdom to God the Father after he has
destroyed all dominion, authority and power. For he
must reign until he has put all his enemies under his
feet. The last enemy to be destroyed is death. For he
"has put everything under his feet."*

—1 Corinthians 15:22-27

This vision of all things reordered properly under God, under Christ's feet, refers to the fulfillment of God's original covenant with creation when humans were commissioned to bring to God everything that was placed under them (Heb. 2:5-9). In the sin of Adam, everything was darkened and disordered. Injustice and death came to dominate. But in Christ the entire creation is reordered and fulfilled. This includes Christ's restoration of humans to their rightful place of stewardly rule, "so that God may be all in all" (1 Cor. 15:28).

We should recognize that humans cannot save themselves and the world by their own political, economic, and scientific efforts. We are not the ones who will bring in the Kingdom of God. But we should also live and work in the knowledge that resurrection to eternal life fulfills children of Adam in the life of the Messiah (1 Cor. 15:42-56). The work of the saints here and now is God's enduring work through us (Phil. 2:12-13). Those who remain faithful to Jesus and die in the Lord "will rest from their labor, for their deeds will follow them" (Rev. 14:13).

The finished work of the Alpha and the Omega is what makes it possible for those who trust in Christ to come to Mount Zion, to enter the new Jerusalem clothed in righteousness, and to celebrate the divine glory and creation's fulfillment. This is what the Spirit showed John.

---

*Then I saw a new heaven and a new earth, for the
first heaven and the first earth had passed away,
and there was no longer any sea. I saw the Holy
City, the new Jerusalem, coming down out of heaven
from God, prepared as a bride beautifully dressed for
her husband. And I heard a loud voice from the
throne saying, "Now the dwelling of God is with
men, and he will live with them. They will be his
people, and God himself will be with them and be
their God. He will wipe every tear from their eyes.
There will be no more death or mourning or crying
or pain, for the old order of things has passed away."*

—Revelation 21:1-4

Justice has been fulfilled. "Amen. Come, Lord Jesus" (Rev. 22:20).

REFLECTING . . .

- Why does Scripture use the politically loaded words *city, new
  Jerusalem*, (Rev. 21:2) and *house* (Heb. 3:2-6; 1 Pet. 2:5) to describe
  the creation fulfilled through Christ's victorious lordship?

- List some of the biblical words and images used to illustrate God's
  perfectly fulfilled kingdom. What is the meaning of images like
  these: "God will wipe away every tear" (Rev. 7:17), "the wolf and
  the lamb will feed together" (Isa. 65:25), "they will beat their
  swords into plowshares" (Isa. 2:4)?

- What kinds of personal and public deeds would express Paul's
  description of the "ministry of reconciliation" as today's "ambassa-
  dors" become "the righteousness of God" (2 Cor. 5:16-21)?

ACTING . . .

- Carry out one of the personal or public deeds identified in the
  discussion of the third reflecting question above.

JUSTICE HAPPENING

Teresita Simbatta stands a little over four feet high. She comes from a community high in the Mountains of Ecuador that's as tiny as she is. She does health training, literacy training, and human rights training with the indigenous people there. Imagine it: women huddled together in blankets with children strapped to their backs, worried about food for today, but studying their rights as women, as people, as land owners. Teresita has brought their cause to the United Nations and to groups all over the world. She leaves her own children at home as she travels the world, speaking of the forgotten indigenous men, women, and children in the mountains of Ecuador. Why? "Because," she says, "there are so many children."

Marion Morgan is from Sierra Leone. Today, that country is ravaged by civil war. A powerful 60-year-old woman, Marion has already far outlived the life expectancy of 43 years. Marion is a peacemaker and realizes that good health means nothing without peace. Yet her organization, the Christian Health Association of Sierra Leone (CHASL), is working steadily at peacemaking and reconciliation where it can. Marion is waiting for the day when they can go back into all communities and work through war trauma. She could retire and live a comfortable life with her husband who teaches in universities around Africa. Why doesn't she retire? Move to a peaceful country? She says, "How could I? So many others are hurting."

Gloria Chavez is from a small rural village in a country the size of Massachusetts. Since the early 1980s, she has been a leader of their local community co-op. But it was a personal tragedy that spurred her on even more. In 1989, Gloria took her baby boy to the city for medical attention. She was told the baby had a hernia, but it could wait to be repaired. Gloria took the boy home, and he died that night. "Why did this happen to me?" she cried. "It's because I'm poor. But this will not happen again to others I know." She kept her promise. Today Gloria speaks to groups of workers in sugar plantations in the Dominican Republic and is working with other non-profit organizations to plan the future work of an international non-government organization in the region. From a tiny village to international venues, from a small co-op in El Salvador to an international organization in the Dominican Republic—all so that disregard for just services will not rob another child from its mother's arms.

What do these three women have in common? They were all brought up traditionally; they were not raised to be activists. Yet they each have a Spirit-led vision of justice fulfilled. They've listened to the call and have been tenacious in living it out. They are prayer warriors and team builders. They know that justice is not about *just us* but about *all of us*.

MEDITATIONS 61-75

- 61 -

THE SECOND COMING

Matthew 25:31-46; 1 Thessalonians 4:13-5:11

"The end is at hand! Armageddon cannot be far away."

You can hear these voices in thousands of churches and read the predictions in dozens of books. Some Christians spend more time speculating about the end times than they do building up the body of Christ for service.

By contrast, at least three things ring out in these two biblical passages from Matthew and Thessalonians. First, when Jesus comes again, he will fulfill God's will for all creation, establishing justice and giving to everyone, both living and dead, what is due them. And this includes gathering God's people to be with him forever in the full inheritance of God's kingdom "prepared for you since the creation of the world" (Matt. 25:34). So we should not waste our time speculating and worrying, but should take comfort in God's promises and "encourage one another and build each other up" (1 Thess. 5:11).

Second, the return of Christ will reveal, both in judgment and in blessing, that the coming age of glory is the fulfillment of life in this age, not the start of another world. Jesus Christ, the Son of Man as well as the Son of God, is the one who will return in glory. The final judgment—his work of separating sheep from goats for eternity, as Matthew portrays it—will be decided, at least in part, on the basis of how people respond to the least of the brothers and sisters of Jesus in this age.

Finally, neither of these passages gives any suggestion that Christians should be trying to "figure out" the timing of the last days. To the contrary, since we do not know when Christ will return, we should concentrate on feeding the hungry and practicing self-control for lives of service in this age so that everyone will be prepared when the end comes.

Many pre-millennial Christians see little continuity between this age and the coming age. They believe that social and political action aimed at restructuring institutions is futile because this world is simply going to be destroyed. On the other hand, growing numbers of postmillennial "reconstructionists" are so convinced that the world will come under the dominion of Christians before Christ returns that they are drawing up plans for how to govern the states of this world theocratically under Mosaic law. Clearly, one's eschatological point of view can lead either to the avoidance of politics or to overconfidence that human efforts can reconstruct the kingdom of Israel as the way to make visible God's authority here and now.

The primary message of the Bible's eschatological passages, such as these in Matthew and Thessalonians, ought to keep us from error. The Lord will bring God's kingdom to fulfillment in due time—in God's time. We will not engineer these events and cannot know the details. At the same time, everything we do here and now, including politics, should be done with the confidence that the King will gather all the good fruits of obedience into the city of God and that justice will be established forever.

REFLECTING . . .

- What is it that most inspires your work and leisure in this age? Does the hope of the fulfillment of God's kingdom play any part in that? Why or why not?

- Read one of the recent popular novels in the "left behind" series by Tim LaHaye or the older book *The Late Great Planet Earth* by Hal Lindsay. What are its implications for politics?

ACTING . . .

- Join a hunger walk, volunteer for a Habitat for Humanity project, become part of a relief effort for flood or tornado victims, or continue your involvement in other works of justice for the "least of the brothers and sisters of Jesus."

So then, let us not be like others, who are asleep,
but let us be alert and self-controlled.

—1 Thessalonians 5:6

- 62 -

HE WILL SAVE HIS PEOPLE FROM THEIR SINS

Matthew 1:18-25; Isaiah 53

Enemies, opponents—they lurk everywhere. Hungry and jobless people face emptiness, and behind their agony may stand a heartless employer or an errant politician. The victim of a mugging soon learns that it happens all the time and that most criminals never get caught.

Individuals are not the only ones to find themselves surrounded by enemies. Iraq's list of opponents is very long today. Israel keeps close tabs on its foes. Tribal wars rage in Africa. Despite the collapse of the Soviet Union, NATO has not disbanded.

Those who have enemies typically want victory or release. They have a deep desire for salvation. Triumph over opponents often feels best because a person or an institution can then enjoy the double satisfaction of retribution and release. The Zealots of Jesus' time wanted him to defeat the Romans and release Israel from its humiliating subordination.

But seldom do nations or individuals admit that their greatest enemy is their own sinfulness. Isaiah and the other prophets told Israel's leaders again and again that the enemy from which they most needed release was not another country but their own disobedience against God. God actually used Israel's enemies—Babylon, Assyria, and Egypt—as tools to try to drive Israel to repentance.

Yet when and how will we finally gain victory over our sin? Isaiah prophesied that the Savior of Israel would be "pierced for our transgressions . . . crushed for our iniquities" (Isa. 53:5). Joseph was told to give the name *Jesus* to Mary's baby "because he will save his people from their sins" (Matt. 1:21).

The people whom God comes to save turn out to be their own worst enemy. The nation that Jesus calls his own will be a new people, released from their sins and drawn together from every corner of the earth into God's final victory over the last enemies of sin and death. Short of God's ultimate triumph in Jesus Christ, there is no release from sin, no victory over disobedience in this age, no justice.

After the suffering of his soul, he will see the light of life and be satisfied; by his knowledge my righteous servant will justify many, and he will bear their iniquities. Therefore I will give him a portion among

the great, and he will divide the spoils with the
strong, because he poured out his life unto death,
and was numbered with the transgressors.

—Isaiah 53:11-12

REFLECTING . . .

- If Christ is redeeming us from our sins, why does it take so long?

- How might the church—the church as a whole, your church—appear to be its own worst enemy to outside observers?

ACTING . . .

- Spend time with a prayer partner confessing personal and national sins and giving thanks for God's forgiveness in Jesus.

For he bore the sin of many, and made
intercession for the transgressors.

—Isaiah 53:12

- 63 -

LOOKING BACK, LOOKING FORWARD

Leviticus 25:8-24; Luke 4:16-19

God's gift of the promised land to Israel occurred in an era when slavery of various kinds was taken for granted. People were often permanently alienated from their land because of conquest by enemies. God's new order for Israel would change this. In liberating Israel from slavery in Egypt, the Lord was reestablishing justice. This meant calling Israel to the remembrance of things past that would help them learn always to look forward to the ultimate fulfillment of God's just order for creation.

The year of Jubilee represents the capstone of remembrance and hope. It is the sabbatical principle multiplied again and again: one day of rest every seven days, one year of rest every seven years, and then the year of Jubilee. Jesus came "to proclaim the year of the Lord's favor" (Luke 4:19), alluding to the Year of Jubilee which pointed ahead to the creation's ultimate, never-ending sabbath.

The people of God must always be looking ahead, marching forward, never trying to hold on to anything in this age as if it could be pinned down permanently. The practice of owning nothing permanently in the promised land was supposed to deepen Israel's appreciation for God's past gifts. At the same time, no one was to be permanently denied the opportunity of owning and caring for their own land. In other words, every family should have its own property on which to learn the habit of sojourning in God's land and looking ahead to the year of Jubilee.

"In this Year of Jubilee everyone is to return to his own property."

—Leviticus 25:13

The only way that everyone can live in the hope of God's final liberation is if each can be a responsible steward of God's gifts in this age and never be enslaved permanently to a human master. Thus, the year of Jubilee required a restoration of past possessions so that everyone would be free again to live in anticipation of God's future blessings and the fulfillment of all creation.

Israel's sabbath pattern can help us understand the meaning of today's realities, ranging from inner-city poverty to South Africa's joyous release from minority rule, from third-world debt to bankruptcy laws. In one way or another, people who have become enslaved to an earthly master need liberation into responsible stewardship—freedom to become tenants of their own property. At the same time, everyone needs to see that release from past bondage in this age does not bring ultimate fulfillment for life but only fuels hope for something more. That *more* is the final Jubilee in God's presence.

REFLECTING . . .

- How can our age of consumerism lead to enslavement to earthly masters?

- Read about the international Jubilee 2000 initiative, which appeals to the rich countries of the world to forgive the debts of the poorest countries. What is good and not so good about this proposal from the viewpoint of Leviticus 25?

ACTING . . .

- Practice responsible stewardship, and teach children how to avoid becoming enslaved to earthly masters.

"Consecrate the fiftieth year and proclaim liberty throughout the land to all its inhabitants."

—Leviticus 25:10

- 64 -

SHAKING THE EARTH

Haggai 2:1-23; 1 Peter 2:4-10

The prophet Haggai addresses Jews who are returning from exile in Babylon. Darius, king of Persia, has given them permission to rebuild the temple in Jerusalem. Looking back to the glory of the first temple as well as forward to the time when God's kingdom will appear in its fullness, Haggai urges the people to trust that God will make "the glory of this present house" (Hag. 2:9) greater than that of the old one.

This is what the LORD Almighty says: "In a little while I will once more shake the heavens and the earth, the sea and the dry land. I will shake all nations, and the desired of all nations will come, and I will fill this house with glory."

—Haggai 2:6-7

Having lived in exile, the humiliated, timid Jews lack confidence. As many prophets had done before him, Haggai reminds them that their God is the one who upholds and disposes of nations at will. The whole earth is in God's hands. The greatest achievements of the greatest nations will be made to serve the purposes of the God who now asks for this humbled people to rebuild the temple.

Today in the United States—or in Poland or China or Iran—people are not busy rebuilding the Jewish temple, to be sure. But if they have any sense at all, they will recognize that God is shaking the earth from one end to the other. While in exile, the Jewish captives might have thought that Babylon or Persia was an unbeatable power, filling the whole earth. Right up until the Berlin Wall fell, many believed that the Soviet Union would endure to the end of time. At different points in recent history, the Ayatollah Khomeini, Noboru Takeshita, and Mikhail Gorbachev each thought he had a firm hold on power.

Suddenly, in a moment, the earth shakes. People throughout the world see nations stumble and great powers crumble. Can anyone doubt that God is shaking the earth, humbling the powers, and calling people everywhere to account?

Where will it all lead? How shall we react to the earth's quaking?

We must learn to number our days and to humble ourselves before the great God who calls us to build wisely. The King of the final, immovable kingdom has already been announced. The chosen One of God now shakes heaven and earth. Through Jesus Christ, God is building the last great temple that will fill the earth and never be destroyed (1 Peter 2:4-10).

So wherever you have your citizenship on earth, seek justice and work for the kind of civic well-being that points ahead to God's kingdom fulfilled. Nothing else will stand. The King is coming; the time has arrived for the Lord of justice to be revealed with his people in all of his glory.

REFLECTING . . .

- Every state or nation holds certain things sacrosanct as representing its permanence. In Great Britain, it might be the monarchy; in the United States, it is probably the Constitution. How do these compare with the temple in Jerusalem and the new temple that God is building in and through Christ?

- What do you think has been the most significant historical event that has shaken the world during your lifetime?

ACTING . . .

- Re-evaluate your civic involvement to see if your modes of action point ahead to God's kingdom fulfilled. Will it stand when the King comes?

"I will overturn royal thrones and shatter the power of the foreign kingdoms."

—Haggai 2:22

- 65 -

OF BUILDERS AND BUILDINGS

1 Chronicles 22:1-19; 28:1-10; 1 Peter 2:4-17

With the growing density of human population on earth, talk increases about whether we can all manage to live here. The talk concerns adequate space and resources as well as sufficient international law and political order within ecological and demographic limits.

Mikhail Gorbachev talked about the "common house of Europe," which he hoped would be built to replace the divided house of the Cold War era. Many environmentalists are more concerned with the future of "spaceship earth" than with the political order of one region or continent. Many homeless people in American cities wish that policy makers would spend as much money on housing as they do on legal fees to handle scandals at HUD (the agency for Housing and Urban Development) or on boondoggles like the savings and loan bailout in the late 1980s.

In this light, it's fascinating to track the biblical story of human and divine dwelling places. From the stone markers in the desert to Solomon's temple, from the land of Canaan to the four corners of the earth, from the Garden of Eden to the holy city of Jerusalem coming down out of heaven, God is present with his people.

This is what the LORD says: "Heaven is my throne and the earth is my footstool. Where is the house you will build for me? Where will my resting place be? Has not my hand made all these things?"

—Isaiah 66:1-2

The apostle Peter, who understood that God had come to dwell among us in Jesus, explained that God's ultimate housing project is a temple composed of human beings, each a precious stone. Jesus Christ is the chief cornerstone, the "living Stone," around which the others are built into a "holy nation" (1 Peter 2:4, 9).

This eschatological vision of justice, of perfect communion between God and his people, does not answer every question about our responsibility today in politics, housing, and worship. But it does put everything in perspective. The work we do here and now, of whatever kind, points to God's larger building project. We must be patient and persevering. Justice is assured. We should build in hope with long-range vision.

The followers of Jesus Christ come from every race and dwell in every corner of the earth. Our good building projects hint at God's larger construction program. Wherever believers live and work, they are being cemented into God's house and thus should concentrate on doing justice, on doing what is right. Living "as servants of God" and showing "proper respect to everyone . . . for the Lord's sake" (vv. 13-17), we look with anticipation to the completion of God's house where we will come home to celebrate together.

REFLECTING . . .

- Even though God calls us to live as sojourners in this age in anticipation of a more permanent home, why is homelessness such a tragedy?

- Jot down five things that are most important about the place where you live. How do these factors help you to anticipate God's eternal dwelling? How might they make your home an idol and endanger your faith?

ACTING . . .

- Visit a homeless shelter and note if any of the five things you consider important about your home are evident there. What can you do to improve the plight of those who come there?

You also, like living stones, are being built into a spiritual house.

—1 Peter 2:5

- 66 -

HEROD THE PROPHET

Matthew 2:1-23; Revelation 11:15

"You've got to be kidding. King Herod, a prophet? No way!"

Look again. When Herod hears about wise men coming from the East to Jerusalem to look for a newborn king of the Jews, he becomes troubled. That is prophetic!

Why should a relatively powerful king be worried about a baby? Why should he pay attention to the behavior of wondering, wandering wise men, even if they are kings in their own countries? Perhaps Herod is simply paranoid. Or perhaps his position is much less secure than one might imagine. But what is prophetic about his worry?

First of all, Herod has done some research and learned from the chief priests and scribes of the Jews that their prophets had foretold the coming of a ruler from Bethlehem. The fact that Herod takes seriously the Jewish prophets is itself a significant hint.

" 'But you, Bethlehem, in the land of Judah,
are by no means least among the rulers of Judah;
for out of you will come a ruler who will
be the shepherd of my people Israel.' "

—Matthew 2:6

Next, Herod begins a search for the child in order to kill him. Somehow Herod senses that this particular child can threaten his throne. Whether Herod knows it or not, he is now entering an arena that transcends ordinary human perceptions and capabilities. Matthew reports that the wise men are warned in a dream not to return to Herod. An angel of the Lord also appears to Joseph, warning him to take Jesus and Mary to Egypt for protection from Herod. Obviously, Herod is up against more than Jews and Eastern wise men; his struggle is with principalities and powers greater than himself.

When he realizes that the wise men have tricked him, Herod orders a mass murder of innocent children across a wide territory. Better to enrage many of his subjects in order to kill the one potential threat to this rule than to give that baby a chance to grow up and unseat him. But Herod's horrible deeds help bring more prophecies to fulfillment (Matt. 2:18) until finally Herod himself dies.

Herod's death brings his prophetic role to completion. Even though Herod's son Archelaus takes over where his father leaves off (vv. 22-23), Archelaus also dies, as will all other rulers on earth. The sole remaining ruler is, and ever will be, this baby who grows to maturity under divine protection, dies on a cross, and is raised from the dead.

Herod, you see, was right. Jesus is the king who will indeed triumph over all kings and take as his dominion nothing less than the whole earth, including Herod's old territory. Matthew's story is about the King of the Jews who has been destined from all eternity to become the King of kings.

That feeling in the pit of Herod's stomach was prophetically on target. He should have been troubled. His throne really did stand in jeopardy. And we who rule or freely vote for governments today should wake up to the enduring truth of Herod's prophecy: The King of kings has made his first but not his last appearance.

REFLECTING . . .

- Think of some examples of rulers today who killed those who might have threatened their hold on power. What, if anything, is new about this pattern in our day?

- What was the political status of the Jews in Herod's time? Why would Herod have felt threatened by a Jewish king? Why would this same Jesus later appear to be a threat to the Jewish authorities?

ACTING . . .

- Meditate on the truth of Herod's prophecy, especially as you feel anxious about today's national and global political scene.

---

*"The kingdom of the world has become the
kingdom of our Lord and of his Christ,
and he will reign for ever and ever."*

—Revelation 11:15

- 67 -

AUGUSTINE AND THE CITY OF GOD

Hebrews 11:8-16; Romans 12:8

In 1986, Christians celebrated the 1600th anniversary of the conversion of Aurelius Augustine. His conversion to Christianity in 386 A.D. had a huge influence on the early Church, an influence that continues to this day. Western history as a whole would not be the same without Augustine.

Politically speaking, Augustine framed most of the fundamental questions that are still in current debate, especially those touching on the limits, norms, and purposes of government in a world corrupted by sin but governed by a sovereign God. In contrast to the Greek and Roman traditions with which he struggled all his life as a philosopher and theologian, Augustine discovered in the Scriptures the historically dynamic drama of a living God at work in creation moving it toward fulfillment in the City of God.

With Abraham, Deborah, Moses, Esther, David, Mary, Paul, and countless other believers, Augustine caught the vision of God's coming kingdom, toward which all of creation moves. His great masterpiece, *The City of God,* directly confronted the declining Roman empire. Rome, like other empires and nations, certainly deserved attention from Christians, Augustine concluded, for this world is the arena of our stewardship before the face of God. Christians can and should be good citizens. No one may rightfully accuse Christians of being the cause of Rome's decline and fall, he argued.

Even so, this age, with all its temporary cities and empires, does not exhaust the meaning of human life. In fact, our lives in this age are meaningful precisely because they are oriented toward a fulfillment far greater than the expansive Roman empire. Augustine, like Abraham, was anticipating the City of God. Christ's death and resurrection secured it.

For [Abraham] was looking forward
to the city with foundations,
whose architect and builder is God.

—Hebrews 11:10

Drawn by this vision of God's coming kingdom, Augustine could see how the whole of history is driven by the conflict between two *loves*. On the one side is self-love—the selfishness which arises from our sinful disobedience against God. Diametrically opposed to self-love stands love for God made possible through the love of Jesus Christ. Because God's love has been given to us through the life, death, and resurrection of Jesus, we may now turn to give ourselves up in service to God and neighbors. Such love creates the community of the faithful, drawing them together even in this age and compelling them toward the City of God.

Those who love God and neighbors will take political life seriously—very seriously—even as they live in conflict with the forces of self-love. But Christians will seek justice in this age, not as an end in itself or out of an idolatrous love for Rome or the United States or Canada, but as subjects of Jesus Christ seeking a higher destiny and longing for the appearance of the City of God ruled by the King of kings.

REFLECTING . . .

- What words written by the apostle Paul remind you of Augustine's distinction between self-love and the love of God?

- In what ways can contemporary interest-group politics manifest self-love? How can a quest for the common good through political action give expression to either the love of God or nationalist idolatry?

ACTING . . .

- During the next election campaign, find out what interest groups the candidates represent, and determine to cast your vote for those who best show love for God and others.

Be devoted to one another in brotherly love.
Honor one another above yourselves.

—Romans 12:10

- 68 -

OVERCOMING RACIAL BARRIERS

John 4:1-42

Jesus walks into the Samaritan town of Sychar, right up to Jacob's well, and addresses a woman with whom no Jew has ever had a conversation. "Will you give me a drink?" he asks (John 4:7).

The woman is as startled as she is intrigued. Quickly she throws up her guard. "You are a Jew and I am a Samaritan woman. How can you ask me for a drink?" (v. 9).

Indeed, how can the iron laws of tradition ever be broken? Jesus, ever so gently, begins drawing her toward his own well. He's not asking her for a drink because he is a revolutionary, defying Jewish laws of purity, or a loose man looking for a way to get a Samaritan woman into trouble. He can ask her for water because behind the hardened traditions that confine Samaritans as well as Jews stands the God who gave the well of water to Jacob in the first place—a gift to serve all of Israel as a small sign of God's larger promises.

"If you knew the gift of God and who it is that asks you for a drink, you would have asked him and he would have given you living water. . . . Everyone who drinks this water will be thirsty again, but whoever drinks the water I give him will never thirst. Indeed, the water I give him will become in him a spring of water welling up to eternal life."

—John 4:10, 13-14

The woman is curious. Maybe this man is not crazy. If he is a magician, she wants to see him work a miracle. She reminds him that he has no bucket for drawing water. How can he give her living water? Does he think he is greater than Father Jacob?

That's the question! Probably unaware of its significance, the woman touches the nerve center of generational longing. Will there ever be anyone greater than Jacob, one who can reunite Israel and overcome the barriers dividing nations? Jesus recognizes the woman's thirst and begins to pour out the precious water of life.

Disputes about where and how to worship God, Jesus goes on to explain, can no longer be used to justify divisions between Jews and Samaritans. The ultimate truth about God's relation to his people transcends both Jerusalem and the holiest mountain in Samaria. Real worship will come alive in God's direct and fully exposing communion—a real love affair—with his people.

"I know that Messiah is coming," she responds, and "when he comes, he will explain everything to us" (v. 25).

Messiah coming? Indeed, he is coming, and he will certainly explain everything. But don't you see? The explanation you've been seeking about Jews and Samaritans, about true worship and eternity, about living water and the history of wells, and yes, about true and enduring love—the truth about all these things is at hand.

"I who speak to you am he" (v. 26).

REFLECTING . . .

- What was the political implication of Jesus speaking to the woman at the well? What question of justice was at stake?

- Think about the land of Palestine today. Why should both the Jews and the Palestinians have a state? Or should they live with equal status in a common state?

ACTING . . .

- Model Jesus' stand for justice by meeting and talking with someone whom others consider an outcast or a "second-class" citizen.

"Sir," the woman said,
"I can see that you are a prophet."

—John 4:19

- 69 -

GOD, THE NATIONS, AND JUDGMENT

Psalm 79; Acts 1:6-8; Revelation 19:11-21

We should know better than to think that the United States, Canada, or any other country can somehow be the specially chosen people of God. The Bible makes clear that the chosen people are not one state among many but the faithful followers of Jesus Christ spread throughout the world. Still, many tend to think of their nation as God's chosen one.

The selected biblical passages above set the issue in proper perspective. Ancient Israel suffered God's judgment because of its failure to be the faithful people God called them to be. The psalmist cried out for God's judgment against the nations that invaded and destroyed Israel, knowing that the devastation was a reproach to God's own name and glory. Bending under God's judgment against Israel, the psalmist pleaded, "How long, O LORD? Will you be angry forever?" (Ps. 79:5).

Pour out your wrath on the nations
that do not acknowledge you, on the
kingdoms that do not call on your name.

—Psalm 79:6

This same plea remained with faithful Jews for generations. Even after Jesus spent years training his disciples, they still awaited the time when God's anger against Israel would abate and judgment would be poured out on the oppressing nations.

As Jesus was about to return to heaven, the disciples asked, "Lord, are you at this time going to restore the kingdom to Israel?" (Acts 1:6). Jesus did not respond with the answer they wanted, but instead gave them their marching orders: go out to all the nations of the earth and tell them who Jesus Christ is. The Son of God did not come to earth to recapture one nation among many for his earthly domain. Christ came to regain the whole world.

When the Lord later gave the apostle John a spectacular vision of how the world would come to judgment, John saw riding on a white horse a man called "Faithful and True" who makes war and judges with justice. His name is the "Word of God" and he leads the armies of heaven against the nations, treading the "winepress of the fury of the wrath of God Almighty" (Rev. 19:11-15).

The message is unequivocal. Even Israel, the one nation God specially chose until the time was right for the Son of God to come in the flesh, was judged and driven out of the promised land for its disobedience. Christ did *not* come to reconstruct Israel; Christ did *not* come to make another nation his special domain. Instead, Jesus came to judge all nations and to reveal the glory of God over the whole earth.

Listen to the word of the Lord, and forget all dreams of special privilege for modern-day Israel or any other nation. We should be awaiting the Lord's return with fear and trembling, knowing that only Jesus Christ can redeem us from the certain judgment that God will pour out on all nations in the process of establishing justice forever.

REFLECTING . . .

• Why did the disciples still question, even to the end of his earthly ministry, Jesus' restoration of the kingdom to Israel?

• Read about Zionism, the movement that led to and helped create the modern state of Israel. Compare the Zionist vision with that of Christians (mostly premillennial dispensationalists) who believe that creation of the state of Israel fulfills biblical prophecy.

ACTING. . .

• Pray for the nations of the world and especially for innocent people who suffer because of warring nations.

On his robe and on his thigh he has this name
written: KING OF KINGS AND LORD OF LORDS.

—Revelation 19:16

- 70 -

DISCIPLINE OR JUDGMENT

Hebrews 3:13; 12:1-29

Do you want temporary pain or permanent oblivion, a refining fire or a consuming fire? That's a tough question for sinful humankind.

The author of the letter to the Hebrews writes with passion and urgency to Christians who need to know the difference between discipline and judgment. A child is not always happy to receive parental correction or reproof. Yet most adults, who look back on constructive discipline received when they were children, can see the love that stood behind it. Healthy discipline, as it turns out, comes from those who can look farther into the future than we can.

On the larger stage of history this lesson has to do with human beings living before the face of God. According to Hebrews, this is still the day of God's grace (Heb. 3:13)—an opportunity for us to correct bad habits, to become mature. As long as it is still "Today," painful discipline may be a sign of God's love that calls us to repentance and reform. So believers ought to be quick to give thanks and to accept such discipline, for it points to an eternity of shalom in God's presence as well as to a more righteous future on earth.

If we refuse corrective discipline, we should know what the consequences will be. They are not pretty. The God who uses refining fire to discipline beloved children is the same God who, when "Today" has come to an end, will act as a "consuming fire" (12:29). When it is no longer "Today," God will cleanse the earth completely. Nothing unruly or recalcitrant will remain.

This message confronts us on more than a personal level. It has everything to do with who we are and how we act in our communities, organizations, and states. As citizens, for example, we should be learning that a government's failure to govern justly demands political reform. We may not blame bureaucrats and politicians, as if they are the sole source of evil. God is telling us—citizens and governments alike—to change our evil ways, as long as we still have time to do so.

The self-righteous, self-seeking, blame-others approach of so much politics today suggests that too few citizens are ready to accept corrective discipline. As a general condition of humankind, this should not surprise us. But Christians? We should be acting in full awareness that "Today" will not last forever. Christians ought to be the kind of citizens most quick to repent personally and to seek the reform of society. In all areas of life we should do as the author to the Hebrews urges.

Therefore, strengthen your feeble arms and weak knees. "Make level paths for your feet," so that the lame may not be disabled, but rather healed. Make every effort to live at peace with all men and to be holy; without holiness no one will see the Lord.

—Hebrews 12:12-14

Our habits in this life have a direct connection to the coming age when we will either flourish as mature and fully disciplined children of God or meet the consuming fire that will burn away all that is unruly and incorrigible. "See to it that you do not refuse him who speaks" (v. 25).

REFLECTING . . .

- Why is it difficult to have a sense of personal responsibility for the shape and condition of the political system?

- Ask a fellow Christian who is active full time in politics—whether in public office or in an organization like the Center for Public Justice—how he or she sees the work for justice coming to fulfillment in God's kingdom.

ACTING . . .

- Where do you see reform most needed in your local community? Plan what you can do alone or with other Christians to begin the process or to continue diligently what has already begun.

God disciplines us for our good, that we may share in his holiness.

—Hebrews 12:10

- 71 -

THE KING AND THE BEAST

Revelation 11-15

On the island of Patmos, the apostle John sees a vision of God's defeat of evil and the fulfillment of all creation through the death and resurrection of Jesus Christ. Chapter 11 announces the blast of the seventh trumpet that follows after the opening of the seventh seal of the great scroll. In chapter 12, John tells us that the enthronement of Christ as Lord of heaven and earth leads to the casting down of all pretenders to the throne—among them the woman and dragon who represent Satan's claim to dominion.

"The kingdom of the world has become the kingdom of our Lord and of his Christ, and he will reign for ever and ever. . . . Therefore rejoice, you heavens and you who dwell in them! But woe to the earth and the sea, because the devil has gone down to you!"

—Revelation 11:15; 12:12

In chapter 13, the mounting drama moves to the earth, where the great beast temporarily inherits the dragon's power. Except for the saints, everyone on earth falls subject to the power of the beast whose number is 666. But the satanic beast is not allowed to gain full control over the earth any more than the evil one was allowed to rule heaven. The triumphant Lamb of God extends his rule from heaven to earth (Rev. 14), giving strength to the saints so they can endure until God has trampled out the grapes of evil on his winepress (14:17-20) and until the final seven plagues complete the judgment (15:1).

We need to see the connection between this revelation and our earthly governments in the full scope of human history. The serpent's lie to Adam and Eve—the earth's legitimate rulers—kicked off the cosmic battle for control of the earth. The legitimacy of human government has never been the question, because God ordained it. But the legitimacy of those who govern has always been a question. When God took Israel out from under Pharaoh, God did not do away with government. Rather, the Lord condemned an evil government and established the framework for a just government.

When Israel's kings misused their office, God again brought judgment—this time on the basis of the very covenant established through Moses. As a result, the prophets began to see ever more clearly the cosmic battle taking place behind the scenes. When the Son of God took on human flesh and became eligible to restore legitimate human rule on earth, the question arose again. Would the second Adam yield to God or to Satan?

Jesus yielded to his Father, was killed, and was raised from death to the kingly throne on high. His divine-human victory now reclaims government for righteousness, and Christ puts his brothers and sisters in positions of authority destined for them from the beginning.

Human government—on God's terms—is a fully legitimate part of creation. Its distortion comes at the hands of usurpers who seek to use its power for evil and not for justice. The beast has no right to rule. King Jesus has redeemed government and will establish just rule forever.

REFLECTING . . .

- Have you ever thought that God's redeeming work in Christ is aimed in part at restoring us to our rightful positions of earthly governance under him? What are the implications of this truth for Christian responsibility today?

- What, if any, signs of righteousness do you see evident in government at the local, state, and national levels?

ACTING . . .

- Encourage your pastor to explain and perhaps to preach on the political significance of Revelation 11-15. Or use *The Day of Christ's Return: What the Bible Teaches, What You Need to Know* (Andrew Kuyvenhoven, CRC Publications, 1999) for a small group in-depth study of Revelation.

"All nations will come and worship before you,
for your righteous acts have been revealed."

—Revelation 15:4

- 72 -
CIVILIZATIONS, MYSTERIES, AND THE END
Daniel 9-12

Civilizations in conflict—nothing new or surprising about that. Nor are we unfamiliar with civilizations rising and falling. But what does it all mean?

Samuel Huntington's now famous argument in *The Clash of Civilizations* helps us see that civilizations, even when we cannot be sure of their exact identities, really do shape history. But his prediction of future clashes between civilizations is ill defined. By contrast, Francis Fukuyama's end-of-history scenario seems to underestimate the potential for the kind of civilizational clashes Huntington sees. Fukuyama prophesies the spread of liberal democracy throughout the world. But whether Huntington or Fukuyama turns out to be right, the consequences will have little to do with the real end of history and the final clash of civilizations.

Many evangelical calendar producers actually claim to be able to unravel the details of the end-time mysteries—mysteries that even prophets like Daniel could not understand. Daniel's prophecy contains many mysterious phrases about sevens, seventy-sevens, time, times, and half a time. These words come as angelic or divine explanations of future developments, some of which have to do with the rise and fall of Persia, Egypt, and other kingdoms.

What strikes one about Daniel's prophecy is his humility and acceptance of his own ignorance as he goes about recording what God shows him. Daniel is confident that God is in control of history even if he cannot make sense of all the visions. He does not write as one presuming to grasp the details about the end of history; he does not try to prove to those of lesser faith and intellect that he has it all figured out.

After seeing a vision of a man clothed in linen above the waters of a river, Daniel says, "I heard, but I did not understand. So I asked, 'My Lord, what will the outcome of all this be?'" (Dan. 12:8). God told Daniel that the words would be closed up and sealed until the time of the end. Daniel should not be troubled.

"As for you, go your way till the end. You will rest,
and then at the end of the days you will rise to
receive your allotted inheritance."

—Daniel 12:13

Here is what I draw from Daniel on this subject: God holds all times, including the end of time, in his hands; when God chooses to disclose the meaning of what Daniel saw, God will do it. In the meantime, we who wish to join Daniel in serving the Lord of history should concentrate more on repentance and seeking to do justice than on the production of speculative calendars and scenarios. Those calendars, like *National Geographic* maps that are now obsolete because of the clash of civilizations, do not seem to last very long.

REFLECTING . . .

• What is it about human nature that leads us to want to know the future? Is it insecurity or desire for knowledge? If God meant for us to live by faith, why are we not satisfied to do so?

• Seldom does one hear Christians in the United States speak about the American empire as one of the great end-time enemies of God or as Babylon or the Great Beast. Yet at this point in history, what "empire" is greater? How does America's anti-Christ role contrast to its positive role in world history?

ACTING . . .

• The next time you turn a page on your calendar, reflect on God's mysterious timing for your life. Be encouraged "to go your way till the end."

"We do not make requests of you because we are
righteous, but because of your great mercy. O Lord,
listen! O Lord, forgive! O Lord, hear and act!"

—Daniel 9:18-19

- 73 -

POLITICS BY FAITH

Hebrews 11:32-40

Hebrews 11 tells of the long tradition of faith-keeping, about those who trusted God for what they could not see and who hoped for what was still not evident. They lived in the confidence that God's promises would be fulfilled, and their example is commended to us.

Part of living by faith is doing politics by faith—"administering justice" as Gideon, Jephthah, and others did (Heb. 11:32-33). Political life either flourishes or becomes oppressive, depending on what and whom we believe. Hebrews 11 gives very little credit to the worldly success or failure of the faithful, but makes a great deal of their faithfulness. Some of the great saints—Joseph and David, for example—enjoyed glory and honor in this age. Others, whose names are not even known, endured calamity.

Others were tortured and refused to be released,
so that they might gain a better resurrection.
Some faced jeers and flogging, while still others
were chained and put in prison. They were
stoned; they were sawed in two;
they were put to death by the sword.

—Hebrews 11:35-37

In the politics of our day, winning and losing can seem to be everything. Those who lose an election appear to have no political future; those who win may gain perhaps only a short future. Our civic attention span is very short, and political life appears to be an entirely this-worldly affair.

For Christians it should be different. We should seek to fulfill our civic obligations in the light of God's revelation in Hebrews. Some of today's political prisoners in China or Iraq or the Sudan may be the final winners in God's scheme of things. Our models should be those who seek justice through faith in God, whether they are prisoners or kings, whether voters or elected officials. True success is the long-range progress of God's covenant-keeping, which may show up in earthly splendor and peace at one moment or in fury and destruction at another.

Politics by faith means working for justice wherever we live, toward the goal of the fulfillment of God's promises, because there is no stopping point short of that. The ultimate goal is not to keep the American economy growing, or to establish democracy throughout the world. No, those who serve God in this age do so in anticipation of a conclusion that will arrive only when all the faithful have completed their work.

That's how the eleventh chapter of Hebrews concludes. All the faithful were commended for their faith, "yet none of them received what had been promised" (v. 39). When Christ returns, all the labors of justice will be harvested together—those of Abraham to those of present-day prisoners, torture victims, and even some North American citizens and public officials. Those who by faith have lived and labored for justice will finally see what they were working for.

_____

REFLECTING . . .

- What is it about our way of civic and political life that frustrates understanding it as part of our Christian life, lived by faith in service to God?

- Compare Hebrews 11:39-40 with Daniel 12:13: "As for you [Daniel], go your way till the end. You will rest, and then at the end of the days you will rise to receive your allotted inheritance." What are the political implications of these passages for us today?

ACTING . . .

- Pray for Christians around the world who are experiencing persecution.

_____

God had planned something better for us so that only together with us would they be made perfect.

—Hebrews 11:40

_____

- 74 -

THE BLESSED HOPE

Titus 2:11-14; 3:8-14

Ever since the resurrection and ascension of Jesus, the remembrance and celebration of Christ's birth have taken on a double meaning. First, we look back at the historical reality of Jesus' birth, and we celebrate Christmas. Second, we look ahead, as Paul says to Titus, waiting for the second coming of our Savior, Jesus Christ.

Jesus has already come, and yet we look forward to his coming. We have already witnessed Christ's incarnation, and now we look forward to the fulfillment of everything he promised. Christmas is more than a memorial birthday party for someone long gone; it is pregnant with a not-yet-revealed future.

In this brief letter to Titus, Paul sends a repetitive emphasis on how believers ought to live in the present age between the two appearances of Jesus Christ. Waiting for the blessed hope is not, in Paul's mind, something to be done passively. Looking forward to the glorious appearing of God cannot be accomplished with an occasional Christmas feast or birthday party, disconnected from the rest of the year's activities. No, Paul again and again tells Titus and his friends that waiting for the blessed hope entails action.

For the grace of God that brings salvation has appeared to all men. It teaches us to say "No" to ungodliness and worldly passions, and to live self-controlled, upright and godly lives in this present age, while we wait for the blessed hope—the glorious appearing of our great God and Savior, Jesus Christ.

—Titus 2:11-13

Time is of the essence, one can hear Paul saying. The second coming of Jesus is not far off, and our lives have meaning because we live in the hope of fulfillment. All the more important then that we build one good work upon another so that there is something to be fulfilled, something to be celebrated in the end.

What should we do with our lives if we have such a hope? We certainly must not waste them in idle speculations and arguments about past genealogies (v. 9) or about the timing of the future. Instead, we should spend ourselves in doing good out of thankfulness for what God is doing through us. "Our people must learn to devote themselves to doing what is good, in order that they may provide for daily necessities and not live unproductive lives" (v. 14).

This has everything to do with politics, our families, our jobs, and our friendships. Everything in all creation is now stamped by the appearing of Jesus Christ—by his first appearance and by the certainty of his return. With that hope, be eager to do what is good and just.

REFLECTING . . .

- How do you understand the relationship or connection between Christ's second coming and the reward or fulfillment believers will receive from the Lord for their "godly lives in this present age"?

- What should government do to help citizens provide for daily necessities and live productive lives? What roles should churches play?

ACTING . . .

- Through prayer, financial gifts, or volunteer work, support a gospel mission program that aims to help those less fortunate become productive citizens and provide for their own needs.

We wait for the . . . glorious appearing of . . .
Jesus Christ, who gave himself for us . . .
to purify for himself a people that are his
very own, eager to do what is good.

—Titus 2:13-14

- 75 -

THE MYSTERY OF THE SLAUGHTERED LAMB

Revelation 5:1-14

The exodus of Israel from Egypt occurred as part of God's judgment on Egypt, a judgment from which God's people were saved only if their doorposts were marked with the blood of lambs. God's final act of redemption also occurs as part of an act of judgment, this time a judgment of the whole world. God's people will be saved from the final judgment only by the blood of the Lamb, Jesus Christ. The mystery of blood sacrificed and of lives saved is great indeed.

The revelation that John receives on Patmos does not resolve the mystery, but rather elevates it to a level of awesome majesty. When the time comes to open the final chapters of history, God shows John that no one on earth or in heaven is qualified to open the scroll. John weeps with the deep pain of one longing for fulfillment, hungry for answers to life's mystery (Rev. 5:1-4).

As he weeps he hears a joyful announcement. Yes, *someone* has been found who is able to break the seals of the last great book! Who is it? It is a slaughtered Lamb. Indeed, precisely because this Lamb has spilt its blood, it is worthy to redeem people from every tribe and tongue and nation. The Lamb is able to make them a kingdom of priests to rule the earth (vv. 9-10).

This language is mysterious; it sounds threatening and dangerous. Is the long history of bloodshed—including Christ's sacrifice—the cause of the crusades and holy wars down to our very day? Do non-Christians have as much to fear from Christians who believe they will one day rule the earth as they have to fear from Muslims who believe that holy wars are required here and now under certain circumstances?

To the contrary, John's vision confirms the message of Christ's Gospel that the final judgment belongs only to the slaughtered Lamb, not to those who slaughter others. Only that Lamb is worthy to receive praise and honor and glory.

"Worthy is the Lamb, who was slain, to receive
power and wealth and wisdom and strength
and honor and glory and praise!"

—Revelation 5:12

The mystery of how God rules from the heavenly throne by means of the slaughtered Lamb is indeed great. But it is a mystery into which we have been invited—not by attempting to enact our own final judgment or by trying to sidestep suffering. Instead, God calls us to fall down to worship the Lamb in praise and adoration and to wait for God to complete all things.

Those who follow Christ may at times find themselves with great power in earthly governments. If their service is marked by Christian character, it will display all the characteristics of humility, modesty, self-control, patience, and love that flow from the Lamb's sacrifice. True Christians wait with John for God to complete the unveiling of the kingdom; Christians will not prematurely seek to establish the kingdom for God.

There is only One who is worthy to open the scroll and to receive praise and honor and glory: the Lamb of God. Justice can now be fulfilled.

REFLECTING . . .

- Why is it sometimes difficult to see government as an office of service—that of public servant—rather than as an imposing beast or violent threat?

- What implications does John's message have for your civic involvement? How can we teach this message to children and young people?

ACTING . . .

- Spend time today in worship and meditation, praising the Lamb of God.

"To him who sits on the throne and to the
Lamb be praise and honor and glory
and power, for ever and ever!"

—Revelation 5:13

A FINAL REFLECTION . . .

While we believe that justice will be done, we can become weary in well doing. Many years ago, Oscar Romero, then the Archbishop of El Salvador, wrote:

> *The Kingdom is not only beyond our efforts, it is even beyond our vision.*
> *We accomplish in our lifetime only a tiny fraction of the magnificent enterprise that is God's word.*
> *Nothing we do is complete, which is another way of saying that the Kingdom always lies beyond us.*
> *No statement says all that should be said.*
> *No prayer fully expresses our faith.*
> *No conversion brings perfection, no pastoral visit brings wholeness.*
> *No program accomplishes the church's mission.*
> *No set of goals and objectives includes everything.*
>
> *This is what we are about.*
>
> *We plant seeds that one day will grow or maybe die.*
> *We water seeds already planted, knowing that they hold future promise.*
> *We lay foundations that will need further development.*
> *We provide yeast that produces effects far beyond our capabilities.*
> *We cannot do everything and there is a sense of liberation in realizing that.*
> *This enables us to do something and do it very well.*
> *It may be incomplete but it is a beginning.*
> *A step along the way.*
> *An opportunity for God's grace to enter and do the rest.*
> *We may never see the results.*
> *But that is the difference between the master builder and the worker.*
> *We are the workers, not master builders. We are ministers, not messiahs.*
> *We are prophets of a future that is not our own.*

> *Stand firm. Let nothing move you. Always give*
> *yourselves fully to the work of the Lord, because you*
> *know that your labor in the Lord is not in vain.*
>
> —1 Corinthians 15:58

ABOUT THE CENTER FOR PUBLIC JUSTICE . . .

The Center for Public Justice is an independent Christian civic education and policy research organization whose work includes the critical assessment of domestic and international affairs and the development of political and policy reforms. Its mission is to equip citizens, develop leaders, and shape policy. Dr. James W. Skillen is the Center's executive director.

This book reflects the work and spirit of the Center for Public Justice and is in keeping with its goals to

- serve God.
- advance justice.
- transform public life.

For more information about the Center and for additional copies of this book and of a separate pamphlet containing the prologue and five essays, contact

The Center for Public Justice
P.O. Box 48368
Washington, D.C. 20002-0368

Phone: 410-571-6300
Fax: 410-571-6365
www.cpjustice.org

Ordering Information
Book: *A Covenant to Keep: Meditations*
on the Biblical Theme of Justice
ISBN 1-56212-544-3
Price: $12.50^{US}/18.15^{CAN}

Pamphlet: *The Biblical Theme of Justice*
ISBN 1-56212-625-3
Price: $1.50^{US}/2.20^{CAN}

(Copies of the book and pamphlet are also available
from CRC Publications, 1-800-333-8300.)
